All that We Are

All That We Are
An Arts And Worship Workbook

* T.E.A.M *
(Theological Expressions In Arts Ministry)
Aimee Wallis Buchanan * Bill Buchanan * Jodi B. Martin

BRIDGE
resources

Louisville, Kentucky

Edited by David M. Dobson
Book interior and cover design by Pamela Ullman
Cover illustration by John August Swanson

First edition

Published by Bridge Resources
Louisville, Kentucky

Web site address: http://www.bridgeresources.org

PRINTED IN THE UNITED STATES OF AMERICA

99 00 01 02 03 04 05 06 07 08 — 10 9 8 7 6 5 4 3 2 1

Library of Congress Cataloging-in-Publication Data

Buchanan, Aimee Wallis, date.
     All that we are : an arts and worship workbook / Aimee Wallis
Buchanan, Bill Buchanan, Jodi B. Martin. — 1st ed.
        p.   cm.
Includes bibliographical references.
ISBN 1-57895-025-2
     1. Worship. 2. Liturgy and art. I. Buchanan, Bill, date.
II. Martin, Jodi, date.   III. Theological Expressions in Arts
Ministry.   IV. Title.
BV10.2.B825   1999
246—dc21
                                                    98-55770

CONTENTS

Acknowledgments

The past seven years have been filled with growth, hard work, blessings, and joy. T.E.A.M. has been surrounded by a host of supporters, friends, advocates, teachers, and fellow artists. Thanks to you all.

We especially thank Paul Osborne for being our mentor and for believing in our vision. His insight and genius in arts ministry have given us a solid foundation on which to build. Thanks to Lynn Turnage, our mentor and friend, who helped us put our vision into action.

Thanks to Gina Yeager, Rodger Nishioka, and Bob Tuttle for their belief that our ministry is important, for their constant advocacy, and for giving us opportunities to minister and grow. Thanks to Melinda Mann for being with us in the beginning when T.E.A.M.'s vision was being formed.

Thanks to all the youth who have served on keynote teams and led our small groups. You, above all, have taught us the most. Your dedication, energy, and spontaneity are sustenance for the journey.

Jodi would like to thank her mother for her wisdom and strength and her father, whose life was an example of perseverance and hope. She especially thanks her loving husband for his calm spirit when disaster strikes and for believing in T.E.A.M. She thanks her children, who are incredibly flexible and full of joy. She also thanks Maxine DeBruyn and Linda Graham Fallon, her dance professors at Hope College.

Aimee would like to thank her parents, Jim and Joanne Wallis, for teaching her how to live her dreams, and Alan Farquhar for convincing her she is called to ministry. Bill would like to thank all the youth directors, advisors, and pastors who have nurtured him on his journey of faith. Aimee and Bill especially thank their daughter for her flexibility, laughter, and unconditional love.

Thanks to our God who calls us to worship with all that we are and who has blessed us with the gift of the arts.

INTRODUCTION

A Theology and Rationale for the Use of Arts in Worship

When we come to worship God, we come with all that we are. We cannot leave parts of us behind. We cannot bring just our minds, just our hearts, or just our physical bodies. We cannot bring our praises without bringing our concerns and deepest needs. Each of us has been created as a whole and connected package.

Since God made us with whole, connected bodies, then it is also with those whole, connected bodies that we are invited to worship, praise, adore, intercess, commune, appeal, honor, and love. In Romans, the Scripture appeals to us to "present [our] bodies as a living sacrifice, holy and acceptable to God, which is your spiritual worship" (Rom. 12:1). The psalmist encourages us to "Make a joyful noise to the Lord" (Ps. 100:1). Jesus taught us that the way to live is to "love the Lord your God with all your heart, and with all your soul, and with all your strength, and with all your mind; and your neighbor as yourself" (Luke 10:27). We are encouraged and even instructed again and again throughout the Bible to worship with all that we are.

Throughout the ages, people have worshiped and praised God with their whole body. Miriam danced. David played his harp. The priests created beautiful temples in which the people worshiped. We watched Jesus express the Word in the art form of storytelling and metaphor. The passion plays of the Middle Ages were a common form of expressing God's story. Michelangelo sculpted David and painted the Sistine Chapel. Many a play, musical, and motion picture has been written to tell the story of Jesus Christ or portray the life of faith. Again and again the arts are present in our expressions of worship to God.

We have been promised that when two or more are gathered together, God is present and active in our gathering (Matt. 18:20). As we consider our own creation, we see how God calls us to be present and active in worshiping. God said, "Let us make humankind in our image, according to our likeness" (Gen. 1:26a). When we have looked at a starry night sky, a beautiful rainbow, a wildflower, or a newborn child, we have seen God's creativity as the ultimate

Creator. If God is the Creator and we are created in God's image, then we were also made to create. Creation is not only who we are, but it is what we are to be about. Using art in worship helps us to worship with our whole creative self. We sing with our voice. We create banners with our hands. We move with our muscles. We hug in a warm greeting. We cry when we are moved by God's presence. We laugh in joy. We dance with all of our body's energy. We act with our feelings.

Art is a wonderful and appropriate medium to use as we come to worship, because art can express all of who we are, what we experience, and how we live. Art incorporates the colors, textures, movement, angles, drama, music, and sounds of life. Art is multidimensional in all of its forms: liturgical movement, visual art, prose, poetry, banners, video, slides, monologues, Reader's Theater, scenes, plays, and so forth. When art is used in worship, worship takes on multidimensions. The flexibility of art provides further opportunities to communicate and celebrate God's involvement in all aspects of our lives.

Art also allows us to express our praise and petitions to a multidimensional God. The Bible presents God in a myriad of metaphors, descriptions, and situations. God is a vibrant, active, colorful, passionate God. Art can help us to reflect God's movement, activity, color, and passion. When we use art in worship, worship becomes that much richer, that much fuller. When worship intersects with our real lives, reflects all that we are, and points to our multidimensional God, we are awakened to God's grace.

Visual media is an effective and familiar way to communicate in today's world. From the creation of the first silent motion picture to the invention of the television to the entrance of the first personal computer into our homes, our culture has become more and more visual. We do not only learn and communicate by the written or spoken word, but also through graphics, charts, symbols, pictures, and stories. The language of today's culture is not only verbal but also visual. Even our e-mail systems, have created a system of visual symbols by using punctuation marks to create pictures. As leaders of worship, we are called to facilitate the people of God in their worship and praise of God. In an increasingly visual culture, the arts not only seem like a viable option, but are, in fact, a necessity if we want to faithfully and effectively facilitate and lead worship.

Liturgical art can be part of any worship service. It does not have to be segregated into a special service, an alternative service, or worship in a retreat setting. Liturgical art can be used in the traditional form of worship that your faith community uses without detracting from the theology or intent of that form of worship. Many denominations provide instruction and guidance about arts in worship through their governing bodies. The Presbyterian Church (U.S.A.) is intentional about offering such instruction and guidance in their Directory for Worship found in the *Book of Order*. You will find the references to art in worship from the *Book of Order* in chapter 8.

All of us have the capability of expressing ourselves through the arts. However, many of us are convinced that we are not artistic by any means. We place artists in a special category apart from average people. We assume that one must be especially talented or naturally gifted in order to be called an artist or to even attempt to do any sort of art. Over the years, we and others have put expectations on our creative selves that are impossible to meet. We have been too hard on ourselves, and often others have stifled us. We have heard messages that have criticized or even denied our creative expressions.

When a child is asked, "Can you paint? Can you sing? Can you dance?" the child naturally exclaims, "Yes!" Sometimes the child shows off the last painting he or she has done. Other times the child breaks out in a favorite song or does his or her own little jig. Painting, singing, and dancing come naturally to the child. However, as the child grows older, she or he changes. When an adult is asked, "Can you paint? Can you sing? Can you dance?" the adult most often answers in the negative: "Are you kidding? I'm a terrible artist. I couldn't draw if my life depended on it. I don't dance and I can't sing." Unfair expectations, critical messages, and hardness of life have piled on the child until the creative self has been smothered. The adult then forgets how he or she once painted, sang, and danced freely as a way of life.

Art in worship is a way to resurrect that part of ourselves that now seems dead. In the resurrection, we are enabled to worship God with all that we are. We are enabled to follow in the tradition of Scripture and the people of God. We are able to express how God is active in the many dimensions and facets of our lives. We are able to communicate the many dimensions and facets of God. We are enabled to use our verbal and visual language. We are empowered to become all that God intends us to be.

An Introduction to T.E.A.M.

Theological Expressions in Arts Ministry (T.E.A.M.) was established by Aimee Wallis Buchanan, Bill Buchanan, and Jodi B. Martin. Each of us comes from backgrounds of drama, dance, music, and visual arts. Likewise we each are called to ministry. As we gathered together and began to talk in 1992, we recognized that there seemed to be a large gap between the church and the arts, yet we did not want to give up one calling for the other. Instead, we each believed that our artistic backgrounds and passions could be used as gifts for ministry. Using the arts could be a way to "speak God's Word" in an alternative language, an intimate language that speaks to the soul as well as the mind. This language is the language of the arts.

As students attending the Presbyterian School of Christian Education (now known as Union/PSCE), we started using our talents to keynote small youth events, church gatherings, presbytery youth retreats, and the like. More recently we have been keynote speakers for the Montreat Youth Conferences and worship coordinators for the Presbyterian Peacemaking Conferences and the Presbyterian Youth Triennium. During the year, we travel to many presbytery youth conferences to keynote through the arts. We also do workshops in churches and presbyteries on how to incorporate the arts in worship.

Our method is to proclaim God's Word and help Christians explore their faith through artistic expressions. Whether it is a drama depicting one of Jesus' parables, a series of monologues and dialogues that wrestle with tough theological questions, or a liturgical dance that visually portrays what our hearts cannot put into words, we help people grow closer to God and discover gifts they never knew existed. We give Christians yet another language to speak to their Creator and each other.

Throughout our ministry we have found that the language of arts is especially appealing to youth. There are many reasons why our method works. We have found that younger generations tend to be more visual than verbal. Youth tend to be more open to alternative forms of worship and study. In addition, T.E.A.M. emphasizes peer ministry. We believe that youth will listen more faithfully and carefully to presentations about faith and God's Word if their peers do the presenting rather than adults. We have seen arts ministry work over and over again as it communicates in meaningful and powerful ways.

Our ministry with youth has two facets. One is the ministry to the congregation assembled. In 1997, we were keynoting our first session for Montreat Youth Conference. Our format was a series of artistic presentations by a youth drama team mixed with storytelling and preaching by the three of us. When we spoke, the congregation did what so many do. They lost focus, leaned on each other in boredom, and caught up on sleep! However, when the youth actors reentered, the congregation gave their full attention, hung on every word, and seemed to feel the power of the message. By the middle of the week, we figured it out. We do not need to speak in a language that bores them when we already have a language that engages them! We let the dramas, music, movement, dance, and visuals do the talking. We spoke in a language that not only engaged their head, but also touched their heart.

The other facet of our ministry with youth is that of enabling. For each conference or retreat that we keynote, we always assemble a new group of actors to be our presentation team. We get to know them. We talk with them about topics and issues facing youth today and get ideas for our scripts. We teach them dramas, dances, and movement pieces for the presentations. Then, when the event arrives, we watch them minister to their peers. Granted, it would be much easier if we were the actors or if we had one group of youth that traveled with us to every event, but then we would miss out on enabling youth, one of the greatest joys of our ministry.

By training and working collaboratively with different youth, we give them opportunities to discover new gifts. Youth who initially seemed shy and withdrawn have turned out to be great actors and preachers of God's Word. Youth who have always felt awkward and insecure have discovered that they are liturgical movers, full of grace and beauty. Nothing excites us more than to hear about a youth on one of our acting teams who has started a liturgical dance troupe at their church, or is still performing dramas for worship. The gift of arts ministry is one to be shared!

The Purpose of this Book

This book is written for adults who work with youth, for youth themselves, and for all people who wish to explore arts in worship and ministry. It is written not just for the experienced dancer, actor, poet, or singer; rather, it is written for those interested in expressing their faith through this mother tongue called art. Whether you are looking for a new method of Bible study, a fresh approach to proclaiming God's Word, or alternate forms of personal worship, we pray that this book will get you started in expressing your faith in new ways through the arts.

1

A Definition of Liturgical Art

Introduction

Too often churchgoers think of liturgy as intricate prayers, long, dry words, or "that language the minister speaks." However, liturgy is supposed to be the communication tool or method of expression that an assembled congregation uses to worship God. Liturgy is the congregation's prayers, praises, petitions, songs, hymns, offerings, and responses to God's good works. Liturgy is intended to be the work of the people—the congregation's intentional response to God.

To be sure, liturgy uses a unique language, the language of faith. However, that language of faith should not be foreign to the congregation, but arise out of the congregation's knowledge and experience of faith. Liturgy is a result of God's work in worship by Christians of the past and present. Too often worship leaders use a language that is inaccessible to many people in the congregation, especially youth and children.

Liturgy need not be aloof, ostentatious, or boring. On the contrary, it should reflect the thoughts, feelings, passions, joys, and concerns of the congregation. It should be a reflection of God's presence and activity experienced by the congregation and the great cloud of witnesses who surround them (Heb. 12:1). When we read about people experiencing God in the Bible, there is nothing aloof, ostentatious, or boring in their experience. The Bible testifies to an experience that is powerful—waters parting, God's hands moving over the darkness, a whole world created by a few powerful words from God, miraculous healings, colorful and rich parables, an array of emotions, and life overcoming death. When we read of people's experience of God in history, we also see God's powerful, intimate activity in their lives. Everything from the Apostle's Creed to the Presbyterian Church (U.S.A.)'s Brief Statement of Faith is a result of people's real experiences of God present and active in their lives. And so our liturgy ought to be also.

In addition, liturgy should be articulated in the language of the people assembled. Sometimes it is necessary for congregations to rewrite traditional prayers into a more modern language so that they might understand what it is they are praying. Sometimes it is necessary to translate a Scripture passage into contemporary terms. For example, it is helpful to imagine who the Good Samaritan might be in today's time in order to communicate a striking relevance to our present situation from a very familiar Scripture passage. However, it is not always necessary to change the wording of liturgy.

Art is a meaningful way to intertwine the language of the people and the language of our faith. Liturgical art is art used in worship. It is art as liturgy.

Reading the Apostle's Creed in unison for many is like reading a foreign language; however, if the reading is accompanied by liturgical movement, suddenly the Apostle's Creed comes alive and is understandable in a way that it was not before. Taking a theological concept such as "justification" and turning it into a banner suddenly makes that complex and abstract concept more real in the lives of faith. When people choose to use liturgical art as part of their liturgy, they are using God's Word, history, tradition, present experience, and creative expression to worship God.

The following process is designed for any group that is exploring the possibilities for arts in worship. The group may be a youth group, youth leadership council, congregational worship planning team, or arts ministry committee. When the group gathers and begins to explore the possibilities of arts in worship, it is important to identify and discuss the definition of liturgical art. The following process will enable the group to create their own definition of liturgical art—that is, art in the liturgy of worship.

Developing a Definition of Liturgical Art

Concept of Worship

Supplies: newsprint, markers, tape

1. Divide the large group into groups of four. If your group is small, you may choose to stay together as one group or divide into pairs. Base your decision on the participants' willingness to share. It may be more comfortable to share if they are in smaller groups of pairs or fours.

Ask each participant to describe a meaningful worship experience in which they have participated. It can be from any worship experience at any time in their lives. Invite them to share when and where it was and identify what made it so special.

2. While still working together in groups of four or pairs, ask participants to create a definition of *worship*. Have the participants write the definitions on newsprint so they can be posted on the wall.

3. Share the definitions in the large group. Post the newsprint sheets for everyone to see. Invite participants to ask questions of each other if they need clarification. After each small group has shared its definition, invite the large group to note differences, similarities, surprises, and new revelations concerning the definitions.

Concept of Art

Supplies: newsprint, markers, tape

1. Ask participants to go back to their groups of four or pairs. Invite the participants to list on a piece of newsprint as many different art media as they can in one minute (movies, plays, paintings, banners, photographs, poetry, etc.). Emphasize that you will be timing them, so they need to think quickly. After one minute, ask the groups to share all the different art forms they have listed. Post the newsprint sheets for everyone to see. After everyone has shared, ask the large group if there is anything else they would like to add.

2. Back in the smaller groups, ask participants to create a definition of art. This definition should be based on the media the group has listed, what they know about art, and personal experience with art in their own lives. Some participants may have trouble with this activity and may want to use a dictionary. However, encourage the participants to base the definition on their own experience and knowledge. Have the small groups write their definitions on newsprint.

3. As with the definitions of worship, share the art definitions in the large group. Post the newsprint sheets for everyone to see. Invite participants to ask questions if they need clarification on the definitions. After each group has shared its definition, invite the large group to note differences, similarities, surprises, and new revelations concerning the definitions.

Concept of Liturgical Art

Supplies: newsprint, markers, tape

1. Invite the participants to go back into their small groups one last time. Ask them to look at the definitions for art and the definitions for worship that are posted on the wall. Invite them to create a definition of liturgical art—art in worship—by combining the definitions of art and worship.

2. As with the definitions of art and worship, share the liturgical art definitions in the large group. Post the newsprint sheets for everyone to see. Invite participants to ask questions if clarification is needed. After each group has shared its definition, invite the large group to note differences, similarities, surprises, and new revelations concerning the definitions.

3. Close the session by asking participants to describe their own meaningful experiences with liturgical art. Let them know that their definitions of liturgical art will be used to guide them as they develop arts ministry in their church or youth group.

2

An Experiential Process for Developing Arts in Worship

Introduction

We want liturgical art in our worship service. We really would like some drama or movement or maybe some banners, but we've never done anything like this before. We just don't know how to think that way or make something work.

The experiential process for developing arts in worship is designed for churches, youth groups, worship committees, and individuals who have ever said any of the above. The process leads participants through several activities that address the obstacles congregations have identified when it comes to the task of developing arts in worship. The activities provide a safe and nonthreatening opportunity for participants to experience and experiment with several art media as they study a Scripture passage. Participants also engage in activities that help them discuss and discover how they might communicate the message of the passage through some artistic form in worship.

Because we are not often given the opportunity to dance, move, paint, sculpt, draw, or write in response to God's Word, this hands-on process uses the teaching tool of experience. When learning about art and worship, the best way to learn is not to sit around and talk about art, but to dive into it. Each person will have the opportunity to explore three art media: movement, visual arts, and writing. Through these activities, it is our hope that each participant might identify the artistic part of who they are.

Everyone is artistic. We make intentional artistic choices every day. When we get dressed in the morning, we make artistic choices as we put an outfit together. When we decorate our homes, we are also making artistic choices. When we choose certain gestures while telling a story, we are once again making artistic choices. These choices are based on color, texture, style, a certain mood, a desired effect, and an intended message. If we can make intentional artistic choices about clothing, decorations, or body language, then we can make intentional artistic choices about worship. The experiential process reminds a group of their everyday experiences with art and artistic choices and, thus, allows a group to see that it is possible to develop their own arts piece for worship, whether it be dance, a banner, painting, or drama.

The experiential process is especially helpful to groups who are at the beginning of their journey with arts and worship or who are not used to approaching Scripture through the arts. However, the process also offers a helpful structure in which to operate for those who are experienced with developing arts in worship, who consider themselves to be artists, or who naturally approach Scripture through an artistic or visual framework.

The experiential process provides an opportunity for a community of faith to gather and work toward a specific artistic expression in worship. Liturgical art is a response to God's grace, presence, and activity as experienced in our own situations, communities, and world. Liturgical art, which is created out of the faith community's unique vision, needs, perspective, and experience, can be powerful. Indeed, it is more powerful than anything that might come out of a professional book where the group simply copies what is on the page. The experiential process helps a community of faith discover Scripture through a new, artistic lens and, in turn, express their discoveries through art in worship.

The experiential process is rooted in Scripture. Worship is turning to God, listening to God, and responding to God. At the heart and focus of worship is God and God's Word. If art in worship is to have integrity and meaning, it must be based on God and God's Word. Liturgical art is never art done for art's sake, but always art done for God's sake. Therefore, the experiential process uses art as a response to God revealed in Scripture. The participants will be able to choose an art form based on their experience of art with Scripture and not just based on their experience with art itself.

The experiential process can be used with any age group, experience level, size, or combination of physical and intellectual abilities and/or challenges. We have used it with youth, intergenerational groups, and older adults. You may have to make adaptations for your specific group. Suggestions for adaptations and variations are given.

The process takes approximately two hours to complete. Time will vary depending on how quickly your group works. If you are limited in time, then an appropriate place to break until the next meeting is after the group has chosen a focus for the message of the Scripture (pp. 19–20). Breaking before that point circumvents the intention of the process to get a group through a Bible study using arts in which they discover a message.

The Experiential Process

A. Entering Activities

Before the group gathers, set up some entering activities around the room. They should be short and simple activities that engage the participant and act as an induction into the subject at hand: exploring arts in worship. Look for great entering activities in chapter 4. Include written instructions with each activity so that the participants can easily move from one activity to the next at their own pace. As participants enter the room, welcome them and invite them to take a walk around the room and begin the activities that you have prepared.

B. Introduction

Gather the group in a circle. You will not need chairs at this time because the next set of activities introduces the group to movement and the room needs to be clear of obstacles. All the activities included in this chapter can be adapted so that everyone—regardless of their ability to stand—may participate.

Briefly introduce the purpose of the meeting. Tell the group that you are going to lead them through a process in which they will explore a Scripture passage with several different artistic media. Tell them they do not need to take notes or evaluate the tasks for future worship activities at this point. This is a time for them to simply experience and learn.

Also, set an atmosphere of comfort and safety. Explain that this is a time to let go and have some fun. Encourage them to affirm each other as they experience new and different things. Also, let them know that there is nothing you will force them to do, if they do not want to do it. Everyone has the option to stand aside.

Supplies Needed for the Experiential Process

For A: Any supplies needed for the entering activities you choose

For C, Activity 1: Upbeat music, tape/CD player

For C, Activity 4: List of concrete and abstract words

For C, Activity 5: A copy of the chosen Scripture passage with highlighted words or phrases

For D: Copy of the Scripture passage with different parts highlighted on each copy

For E: Soft, instrumental music, CD/tape player, tables and chairs, art supplies (playdough/clay, colored pencils, crayons, markers, glue, construction paper, scraps of wrapping paper or construction paper, scissors, paints, canvas, fabric scraps, magazines [for collages], newsprint [or other large sheets of paper], beads, leather string, glitter, and any other miscellaneous items you can find in the church supply closet)

For F: Paper and pens/pencils

For H: Newsprint, markers, and tape

For K: Newsprint, markers, tape, a person to take notes

C. Liturgical Movement

The first art media the group will explore is liturgical movement. This process takes a group from playing games to actually creating and participating in liturgical movement to the Scripture passage you have selected.

1. Mingle/Mingle

Supplies: upbeat music, tape/CD player

Invite people to mingle. They should say "hi" and shake hands as they walk around the room while the music is playing. When the music stops, ask the participants to each find a partner (the person standing closest to them) and introduce themselves by name. Then have the participants ask their partner a question, such as:

- If you could go anywhere in the world for a vacation, where would you go?
- If you could choose three musical artists for a concert, who would they be?
- Who is your favorite Bible character (besides Jesus)?
- If Jesus were to come back today, what kind of music would he listen to?
- If you could recommend one book to the world for required reading, what would it be?

After doing the activity as instructed a few times, invite participants to mingle around the room, but this time, ask them to walk in different ways (first using the largest steps they can make, then in small steps, backward steps, fast steps, slow steps, and/or silly or goofy steps).

2. Mirror, Mirror

Ask each person in the group to find a partner and choose who will be the leader first. Ask partners to face each other, standing about a foot apart, and hold hands up to each other without touching. Tell them they are each other's mirror image. When you say "Go," the leader of each pair will begin to move and the partner will follow. When you say "Switch," the follower becomes the leader. A helpful tip: It is easier for the follower if he/she uses peripheral vision to follow both hands at the same time by looking in the center of the leader's chest or in their eyes instead of trying to follow each hand individually. The leaders are free to move hands, legs, and so forth, but the object is for the partners to work together, not to trick each other.

After a few moments, ask the partners to stop and identify what it is they are doing well and how they could accomplish the task with even more success. Have them try it again.

3. Balancing

Invite the pairs to turn back to back and lean in on each other. They may slowly inch their feet forward to see how far back they can lean on each other. Encourage them to try balancing together in other positions: facing each other with arms and hands extended in front, shoulder to shoulder, and so forth.

Then invite the pairs to stand face to face, holding hands and pulling away from each other. They may slowly inch their feet forward to see how far they can lean out without falling. Encourage them to experiment with different positions and difficulty again, such as side to side, holding on to each other with hooked elbows or clasped hands, back-to-back leaning forward with clasped hands behind them, and so forth.

As the leader, it is your job to create an atmosphere of safety. The object is not to trick the partner or to make them fall, but to work together as a team.

Once the participants have had an opportunity to work with their partner, invite the pairs to join with another pair to create groups of four. It is important to repeat the balancing exercise to help develop trust among group members. Allow the groups of four to experiment by pushing and pulling on one another.

4. Sculpture Garden
Supplies: list of concrete and abstract words

While still in the same groups of four, ask each group to stand facing each other in a circle. Tell the groups that they will be forming a sculpture garden and that each small group will be one of the sculptures in the garden. Tell the group that you are going to call out a word and count to five out loud. In those five beats, the group should move into a sculpture. There are three rules: (1) No one can talk or instruct the group. (2) Each individual must be touching at least one other individual. (3) There is no right or wrong sculpture. Just do what comes naturally.

Begin with concrete words such as "lighthouse, volcano, tree, wave, church, mountain, and so on." Then move to more abstract words such as "joy, fear, anger, love, baptism, communion, and worship." After you say each word and the group has done the sculpture, ask the group to return to their circle facing each other to do another sculpture. They should always start from the circle.

After the group seems comfortable moving into sculptures, try some of the following variations:

- Ask participants to take five steps away from their starting place. Now repeat a previous sculpture word and invite them to walk toward one another. They should begin to form the sculpture as they step inward.
- Ask participants to move into the sculpture by starting in the circle with their backs to each other, then turning toward each other as they make the sculpture.
- Ask the participants to move into a sculpture one at a time when you call out a word.

- Ask the groups to freeze in their sculptures. Then let one group at a time relax and look at the other sculptures. Invite them to walk all the way around each sculpture. Doing this activity is especially interesting when the groups have formed different sculptures for the same word.

Invite the groups of four to join another group to form eight. In these larger groups, repeat some of the concrete and abstract words so that they make new sculptures with the larger group. However, this time, instead of breaking out of each sculpture to begin a new sculpture, the group should move from one sculpture to the next as you call out the words. Encourage the groups to try becoming parts of a whole instead of eight individuals doing eight separate poses for words such as "anger" or "joy."

Sculpture groups should never be any larger than eight people. If you have 8–10 people in your whole group, you may leave them in groups of four instead of forming groups of eight. If your whole group is no larger than 5–6 people, have them combine the pairs into the whole group.

5. Scripture Sculptures
Supplies: a copy of the chosen Scripture passage with highlighted words or phrases

Staying in the same groups of eight, the groups will now form sculptures to words you have chosen in advance from a Scripture passage. The Scripture should be chosen from something that will be used in a future worship service or that you would like to use in a future worship service. If you are using a psalm or something expository from the Epistles, choose a list of vivid words from that passage. If you are choosing a story, it is especially helpful to use the action verbs and adjectives/adverbs from the story. In some cases, it may be necessary to choose a phrase from the story instead of just one word. If the passage is especially long, you may want to pick only one word per verse or only work on one section at a time. Below are some examples of Scripture with highlighted words.

> *Our Father,* who art in heaven,
> *hallowed* be thy name.
> Thy *kingdom* come,
> thy will be done,
> on *earth* as it is in *heaven.*
> *Give* us this day our *daily bread.*
> And *forgive* us our debts,
> as we forgive our debtors.
> And lead us not into *temptation,*

but *deliver* us from evil.
For thine is the kingdom,
and the *power*,
and the *glory*, forever.
Amen.

   —The Lord's Prayer, KJV

I consider that the *sufferings* of this present time are not worth comparing with the *glory* about to be revealed to us. For the creation *waits with eager longing* for the revealing of the children of God; for the creation *was* subjected to futility, not of its own will but by the will of the one who subjected it, in *hope* that the creation itself will be set free from its *bondage* to decay and will obtain the *freedom* of the glory of the children of God. We know that the whole creation has been *groaning in labor pains* until now; and not only the creation, but we ourselves, who have the first fruits of the Spirit, *groan inwardly* while we wait for *adoption*, the *redemption* of our bodies. For in *hope* we were saved.   (Rom. 8: 18–24a)

A large crowd followed him and *pressed in* on him. Now there was a woman who had been *suffering* from hemorrhages for twelve years. She had *endured* much under many physicians and had *spent all that she had*; and she was no *better*, but rather grew *worse*. She had heard about Jesus and came up behind him in the crowd and *touched* his cloak, for she said, "If I but *touch* his clothes, I will be *made well*." Immediately her hemorrhage stopped; and she felt in her body that she was healed of her disease.   (Mark 5:24b–29)

Tell the group that you are now going to read a new list of words. The same process will be used: say a word, then count to five while the groups move into a sculpture and then stop at the count of five. However, this time, instead of breaking the sculpture after they finish and starting again from a circle, the groups should hold one sculpture and move from it to the next sculpture. Say the list of words that you chose in the order that they appear in the text. Have the group do sculptures to the first few words and then repeat the words and have them do the sculptures again. The groups may change their sculptures each time the list is read or they may keep them the same. Repeat this process until you have gone through the entire list. Eventually, through this stop and repeat process, the groups will settle on a sculpture for each word.

Now explain that the words you have used come from a Scripture passage. Tell them that you will now read the Scripture and when one of the words appears in the passage, you will pause so that the groups can make their sculpture. Make sure to read the passage slowly, emphasizing the key words. Read the passage a second time and invite the group to change any of the sculptures now that they have heard the context in which the word appears. Read the Scripture passage once more, allowing the group to move on its own initiative and rhythm.

Now the groups are doing liturgical movement to a selection of Scripture! Invite the groups to share their movement pieces with each other. Remember that there are no right or wrong movements. The sharing is simply for the groups to enjoy one another and gain new perspectives from being an observer in the sculpture garden.

Before the group continues to the next activity, take a moment to discuss the following questions. (Remember, this is not the time to begin a long debriefing session, but a time to mark the moment.)

What did you like about the sculptures?

Was there anything surprising or new in the movement you saw?

As you did your own sculptures and as you watched others do theirs, did anything strike you about the sculpture?

Did you see something new or different in the Scripture?

D. Dividing the Text

Supplies: copies of the Scripture passage with different parts highlighted on each copy

Before the meeting, divide the Scripture into verses, lines, or sections. If you are using a story, you may want to divide the passage by characters. Make copies of the Scripture passage and on each copy highlight a different part. After you have finished the sculptures, give each person in the group one of the copies with different highlighted verses, lines, sections, or characters. It is helpful to give out the full passage with individual parts highlighted, instead of a sheet that has only a part of the Scripture, so that the participants can see their part as it appears in the context of the whole passage. Also, later they will be able to refer to other participants' parts in the sharing time.

E. Visual Art

The second art media the group will experience is visual art: painting, drawing, textiles, coloring, sculpting with clay, and so forth. Before the group meets, you will need to have gathered several art supplies (listed below). They should be arranged on tables that can easily be pulled into the center of the room after the movement section is completed. It is important that this section begin with a period of silence where the participant contemplates their verse, line, section, or character from the Scripture.

Silence and Visual Symbol/Response
Supplies: soft, instrumental music, CD/tape player, tables and chairs, art supplies

Invite the participants to silently and individually meditate on their part of the Scripture. Ask them to:

- think about it
- pray about it
- note what questions arise as they read it
- note what feelings they experience as they read it

Tell them that in five minutes you will begin playing some quiet music. When they hear the music, it is their signal to move to the tables and begin creating a visual symbol or response to their part of the Scripture by using the supplies on the tables in the room. The visual symbol or response could be a realistic drawing of what is described in their passage or an abstract sculpture of a question they have about their part of the passage. They simply need to respond to their part of the passage in whatever way seems fit. Encourage the participants to stay away from writing words, as writing will be the focus of the next section.

Often you will have to be the coach and encourager for participants in the group who are intimidated by this activity. Try not to give them specific ideas as to what they should draw or paint but listen to them and encourage them to think about the questions they contemplated in silence. Often people will say, "Well, I'm not an artist." Your response should be, "The point is not to show your artistic ability, but to simply respond to the Scripture."

It is helpful to allow at least ten to twenty minutes for creating their visuals. In any case, explain how much time they will have and give time warnings as the exercise continues. Make sure to give the instructions about making their visuals before silent time, so they can move from silence to creating their visual without interruption.

The art supplies should be many and varied. It is helpful to have many different media available so that participants can explore the options and find what best suits them and their passage. Arrange clay, colored pencils, crayons, markers, glue, construction paper, scraps of wrapping paper or construction paper, scissors, paints, canvas, fabric scraps, magazines (for collages), newsprint (or other large sheets of paper), beads, leather string, and glitter on the tables as well as any other miscellaneous items you can find in the church supply closet.

After time has expired, ask the participants to share their visual symbols and responses in their movement groups. Remind participants that they can share as much or as little as they want.

F. Writing

Having experienced the Scripture through liturgical movement, silence, and visual art, the group will now experience the Scripture through one more artistic media: the written word. As the participants are still sitting in their movement groups and after they have shared their visual symbol/response, begin the next activity.

Free Writing
Supplies: paper, pens or pencils

Give each participant a pen or pencil and piece of writing paper (they may also write on the back of their Scripture sheet). Explain that free writing is a process of writing whatever comes into your head about a certain subject at a certain time. Therefore, for the purposes of this exercise, invite the participants to write whatever comes into their head at that moment about the Scripture passage at hand. Allow at least five minutes, but make sure you tell the group before they begin exactly how much time they have. When time has expired, ask them to finish the sentence they are on and put down their pens or pencils.

Invite the participants to share their free writing in their movement groups. Remind participants that they can share as much or as little as they want.

G. Break

At this point, it is helpful to take a break. The experiential process is finished and the break provides the transition into the working session that follows.

H. Reflection Time

Supplies: newsprint, markers, tape

Gather the group together, either sitting at tables or in a circle. The following activities and discussion questions are meant to help the group debrief the process they have just completed, reflect on it, and make some specific choices for worship. You will need newsprint and markers throughout the rest of the process.

1. Debriefing
After the group has gathered, ask the following questions in the order they are given:

- What were the activities we did starting from the time you walked in the room?

(List the activities from beginning to end on newsprint so that the group can see and refer to the whole experience. Tape the newsprint on the wall.)

- What did you like best?
- What did you like least?
- What were you thinking as we did these activities?
- What were you feeling as we did these activities?
- What did you learn about the Scripture?
- Is there something new that you saw/heard in the Scripture?
- What questions do you still have about the Scripture?

2. Exegetical Concerns

Exegesis refers to pulling out the meaning of a passage. Exegetical concerns include language usage, historical context, location within the whole of the canon, literary genre, and immediate context. The experiential process is not intended to exclude the exegetical process, but to allow for an initial experience of the passage through the arts. At this point, the group should do some exegetical work. Refer to pp. 26–27 for options on how to do this.

3. Choosing a Focus
Supplies: newsprint, markers, tape

First, ask the group about the message of the Scripture. Invite them to put it in a word, phrase, or one sentence. As people begin to share their words, phrases, and sentences, write them on newsprint. In order for the group to get a sense of what everyone experienced and thought, keep this as a brainstorming session where all contributions are put on the newsprint. Post the newsprint on the wall.

Second, ask the group what is important to communicate about the passage. Perhaps it is the beauty of the words, the message itself, the power of the story experienced visually, or an incredible metaphor. Also write these on newsprint and display them on the wall.

Third, ask the group to take a moment to look at all the different newsprint sheets on the wall. Ask the group to focus on what message they would like to present or what is important to communicate about the Scripture. It may quickly become clear or the group may have to work a little harder. However, it is important that the group make a decision of some sort. Remind the group that they may not be able to communicate everything about the Scripture (especially if the conversation has been rich, full, and diverse), but instead highlight a specific focus (especially if there are certain time limitations in worship to consider). After the group has chosen a certain focus, write it on a piece of newsprint and post it on the wall.

4. Choosing an Art Form

Now that the group has chosen the focus, they are ready to explore what art form would best communicate what they want to share. Start by reviewing the different art forms experienced in the process they just finished (liturgical movement, visual art, writing). Write them on newsprint and then add to the list other art forms that are possible (banners, video, slides, different kinds of drama, etc.).

Ask the group to look at the chosen focus and the list of art media. What looks like an appropriate art form to communicate the chosen focus? What excites them? Through the discussion, the group should choose the art form they will use.

The group is not limited to one art form. They may choose a multimedia format. For instance, they could begin with a slide show that leads into a liturgical movement piece that leads into a drama. But be careful. If the group is just beginning, we recommend choosing a goal that is the most attainable and has the most likely degree of success. It would be devastating for a new group to create a high goal that they could not complete or that turned out to be a huge burden instead of a blessing. A runner does not begin with a marathon, but rather with months—even years—of training.

5. Developing an Arts Piece for Worship

Now that the group has chosen the art form and has their focus, it is time to develop the idea. Help them answer the following questions:

- What are our time and space needs? What are our time and space limitations?
- How long will it take to accomplish the task?
- What are the needs and abilities of the group?
- What do we need to make this happen (a script, a big piece of canvas, a stage, etc.)?
- Who do we need to make this happen (writers, painters, actors, movers, etc.)?

After answering those questions, complete the following tasks:

1. Make a time line. Start with the date of the performance. Now back up. How much time will you need in rehearsals or work time to be ready for the date of performance or sharing? What do you need to do before you can start rehearsing (develop a script, etc.) or working (gather supplies for the

banner, etc.)? Answering these questions should help you decide how much time you need and, thus, on what date the time line should begin.

2. Make a recruitment list of people whom the group will ask to help them with the project. The group itself may do the work, be the actors, or do the liturgical movement. Or the group may need to ask others to help.

3. Secure the room where you will work and rehearse, as well as time for a few rehearsals (if not one dress rehearsal) in the space where you will perform. Also, decide if it is necessary to secure the space where you will perform (if it is not during worship).

4. Make a supply list. What will you need? Who is going to get the supplies?

5. Make decisions about publicity. If you want or need to publicize, how will you publicize? Who will do the publicizing? Also, how will you publicize the rehearsal/work dates? Who will send out reminders of rehearsals/work dates to those involved?

6. Choose a coordinator. It is important that one person in the group be the clearinghouse for all of the above tasks. That person should not be responsible for doing the tasks (writing the script, doing the shopping, etc.), but instead should be responsible for coordinating and making sure everything is running smoothly. With a task that involves so many people, it is important to have a coordinator.

I. Prepare and Rehearse

Make the best use of your rehearsals by being prepared and on time and encouraging others to do the same. Here are a few things to think about:

- Send out reminders of rehearsal/work dates and times that include the specific task you will be working on and what is expected of the participant (having the first half of the script memorized, wearing loose clothing for movement or clothes that can get dirty for banner making, bringing a certain supply, etc.).
- Be a good steward of your time and that of others. Keep the group focused on the task by being fully prepared yourself, otherwise rehearsal and work time will be stalled and the participants will lose focus and energy.
- Have the workspace or rehearsal space ready for work and rehearsal (chairs moved, tables set up, etc.).
- Have all supplies ready and available.
- Begin and end each work session and/or rehearsal with prayer in thanks for God's presence and faithfulness and a thank you for the participants' work, energy, and commitment to the task.

J. Performing/Sharing

The time to perform the drama or liturgical movement piece or share the banner or other visual art has arrived. Are you ready? Sure you are. You've worked hard and the moment has arrived.

Remind those involved that the reason and inspiration for the project is to glorify, praise, and worship our Creator God. The performance or sharing is not only for the people who see it, but more important, it is for God.

Plan a celebration to be held after the performance or sharing where all the participants may gather together. You may want the celebration to include only the group who worked on the project or you could invite the whole congregation to a reception after the performance/sharing. Celebrate your hard work. Thank God for God's steadfast love and faithfulness in all that we do.

K. Evaluate

Supplies: newsprint, markers, tape, someone to take notes

Gather the group together for an evaluation session. Write notes and ideas on sheets of newsprint and post the sheets on the wall so the group can get the overall sense of the evaluation. Also, designate someone to take notes during the discussion. You may want this person to be from outside the group, so that everyone else may participate fully. Discuss the following questions:

- What did we do well at the performance/sharing? What could we have done better?
- What did we communicate?
- What did the congregation feel/think?
- What did we feel/think?
- What went well at work times and rehearsals? What could we have done better?
- How was the planning process?
- What should we keep doing?
- What do we want to do next?

3

A Deductive Process for Developing Arts in Worship

Introduction

The process outlined in this chapter is a more deductive and less experiential way of getting a group or individual to develop an arts piece for worship. Instead of working with a Scripture through hands-on activities with different art media, the participants will sit together at a table, read Scripture, and participate in a discussion to help them make choices about arts in worship.

The deductive process is meant for people who are already experienced with art and using art in worship. This process is helpful for groups who have used the experiential process several times. After the group has experienced approaching Scripture and themes from an artistic framework, they will be ready to move to something new.

The deductive process also takes less time than the experiential process. Because of the experience the participants bring to the table, they are able to move more quickly from the study of Scripture to the implementation of artistic ideas.

The deductive process can be used with any Scripture passage. It can also be used with a certain theme or subject matter (such as faith, forgiveness, sin, etc.) that the group wants to use in worship.

Supplies Needed for the Deductive Process

For A: Any supplies needed for the entering activities you choose

For B: Any supplies needed for the group-building/trust-developing activities you choose

For D: Bibles, pens/pencils, paper

For E: Copies of the exegetical study or Bibles, pens/pencils, paper,

exegetical resources such as commentaries, language dictionaries, different Bible versions, textbooks, articles, etc.

For F: Newsprint, markers, tape

For G: Newsprint, markers, tape

For K: Newsprint, markers, tape, someone to take notes

The Deductive Process

A. Entering Activities

Before the group gathers, set up some entering activities around the room. They should be short and simple activities that engage the participant and act as an induction into the subject at hand: exploring arts in worship. Look for great entering activities in chapter 4. Include written instructions with each activity so that the participants can easily go from one activity to the next at their own pace. As participants enter the room, welcome them and invite them to take a walk around the room and begin the activities you have prepared.

B. Group-Building

Gather the group together and participate in one or more group-building or trust-building activities. It is important that the group reacquaint themselves with each other. You may feel this is unnecessary for the group that has been working together for a while. However, "reacquaint" does not mean that they need to remember each other's names, but they need to catch up with each other, remember what it is like to work together, and learn more about each other. The group also needs to continue in growth by intentionally working together on issues of group-building and trust. There are several excellent activities for this purpose found in chapters 5 and 6.

C. Introduction

Briefly introduce the purpose of the meeting. Tell the group that you are going to lead them through a deductive process that will help them study and explore a Scripture passage or theme in order to develop arts in worship.

D. Introducing the Scripture or Theme

Supplies: Bibles, pens/pencils, paper

1. Introducing the Theme

The introduction of the theme will lead to identifying what Scripture the group wants to use. After the group chooses their Scripture, they will then need to do the activities below for introducing the Scripture. Introducing the theme and introducing the Scripture are two processes that could take a long time. If you are starting with a theme introduction, you may want to schedule a preparation meeting where the group simply deals with introducing the theme and introducing the Scripture. Then meet again to complete the rest of the deductive process.

Once the group is gathered and ready to begin the introduction of the theme, ask someone to review the meaning of the theme that has been chosen. Allow time for the group to discuss and ask questions to clarify the meaning and intent of the theme.

Next, ask the group to put the meaning and the purpose of the theme into one sentence or phrase. You may do this as a whole group or in pairs or groups of three. Ask the groups to share their sentences and phrases. Give everyone in the group a chance to ask more questions for clarification. Allow time for discussion.

After the group has explored the theme, ask them to brainstorm Scripture passages that might fit the theme. Encourage them to think of specific stories, psalms, parables, commandments, instructions, and situations in the Bible that seem to fit with the theme. After they have shared, ask them to examine their lists, answering the following questions: What passages seem particularly applicable? Which ones excite the group the most?

Once again ask the group to examine the passages until only a few are left. How many can they use? Are the ones on the list connected in any way? Remind the group of the meaning and purpose of the theme. Also remind them of their time limitations both to prepare and perform/share their arts piece. Tell them that the more focused they are, the easier it will be for them to work and for the congregation to understand. Select one passage (or two if they connect) to use.

2. Introducing the Scripture

First, ask the group to open their Bibles to the Scripture that has been selected. After everyone has found the passage in their Bibles, ask the group to take a deep breath and then exhale slowly. As they breathe out, encourage them to clear their head and focus on the Scripture they are about to read. Next, read the Scripture while the group follows along in their own Bibles.

After your first reading, ask the participants to close their eyes. Tell them you are going to read the Scripture again. Ask them to imagine that they are there in the situation, the time, the story, or the passage. Read the passage a second time. Read slowly, so that the participants have time to concentrate and imagine they are a part of the passage.

After your second reading, ask them to keep their eyes closed. Tell them you are going to read it one more time. Ask them to listen for one word or phrase that strikes them as they hear the passage, concentrating on that one word or phrase after they hear it. Encourage them to focus only on the one word or phrase. Tell them there will be a time of silence after the reading to meditate on the word or phrase they picked. After you finish reading the

Scripture and as they meditate, ask the following questions:

- What is God saying to you through the Scripture word or phrase you picked?
- How is God comforting you?
- How is God changing you?
- How is God challenging you?

If it is helpful for your group to open their eyes and do some free writing, they may. Instructions on free writing are found in chapter 2 (p. 18).

After your third reading and three to five minutes of silence, ask the group to open their eyes and focus back in as a group. Take time to discuss the following questions:

- What were you thinking as we read and listened to the Scripture?
- What were you feeling as we read and listened to the Scripture?
- What did you learn about the Scripture?
- Is there something new that you saw/heard in the Scripture?
- What questions do you still have about the Scripture?

E. Studying the Scripture

1. Exegesis
Supplies: copies of the exegetical study for the passage or pens/pencils, paper, exegetical resources such as commentaries, language dictionaries, different Bible versions, textbooks, articles, etc.

Exegesis refers to pulling the meaning of a passage out of the passage itself. Exegetical concerns include language usage, historical context, location within the whole of the canon, literary genre, and immediate context.

There are many ways to handle this job. You could do the research or ask a person(s) to do the research before the group gathers. Ask that person to present the information to the group. If the passage you have picked is the passage the pastor will be using for his/her sermon, you could ask him/her to give you their exegetical notes. You could also divide the group into pairs or smaller groups during the meeting and have each group answer one of the exegetical questions that follows. Base your decision on the amount of time you have at the meeting, the resources that are available to you, and how much work can be done beforehand.

If you will be studying together as a group, provide resources such as commentaries, language dictionaries, textbooks, different Bible versions, and articles on the passage or the book from which the passage is taken. As you begin your study, answer the following exegetical questions. Share your answers with each other, making sure to allow time for questions and discussion.

- Are there any special nuances or definitions of words? Pay attention to the Greek or Hebrew definitions of words. If there is anything special to note from the Greek or Hebrew, you will usually find it highlighted in commentaries on that particular passage. Look at different Bible versions. What are the language differences? Why are there differences? What insights do you get from the language?

- What is the historical context of the passage? What were the cultural norms and practices of the time that might have affected what happens in the action of the passage, what language is used, or the way the author has written the passage? What insights do you get from the history and culture?

- Is there any significance to where the passage appears in the Bible? Is it part of the Pentateuch (the first five books of the Bible), the Gospels, the Prophets? What insights do you get from where the text appears in the canon?

- What is the literary genre of the passage? Is it a psalm, a story, a parable, a proverb? Does the literary genre tell you anything about the author's intent?

- What is the immediate context of the passage? How does what happens before and after the passage affect what is in the passage? Also look at it from the opposite direction: How does what happens in the passage itself affect the immediate context? What insights do you get from the context of the passage?

2. God's Message

Before the group moves to the next activity, take a moment to discuss the following questions. This is not the time to make final decisions about the message of the passage, but a time to mark the moment by identifying what is presently striking the group about the Scripture.

- What is God doing in the passage? What is God's action?
- What are the characters or words saying about God?
- What is God's message to the characters or to the people of the time?

3. Searching the Scripture

In pairs, small groups, or as a whole group, identify the following things that are found in the Scripture passage.

1. What are the concrete verbs or actions in the passage? (he walked; she said; he touched)

2. What are the abstract verbs or actions in the passage? (he felt; she praised)

3. What are the images or pictures in the passage? (mountains; a crying father; a furious Pharisee)

4. What is the mood of the passage? What are the characters feeling? What

do you feel as you read it? (fear; excitement; awe; wonder)

5. What metaphors or similies are in the passage? (God is like a mountain; we are lights)

4. Five Senses

Look for the five senses found in the Scripture passage. Let your five senses experience the passage. You may divide into pairs or small groups each with a separate sense on which to focus or you may discuss all the senses as a whole group.

Sound. What sounds are in the Scripture? (the tearing of cloth; the crying of a woman; the gasp of a healed person) Listen to the Scripture again. What words strike you now? What do you hear that is new or different?

Touch/Movement. What textures are in the passage? (a rough blanket; hay; rich silk) What are people doing with their bodies in the passage? (a touch of love or healing; crouching in pain; standing straight in haughty anger)

Imagine doing a movement piece to the Scripture passage. How would you move? Who would be in the movement piece? If you have time, do an improvisational liturgical movement to the passage.

Sight. What do people see in the Scripture passage? What visual images are present or described? (mountains; Jesus; the cross) What is visually happening in the story? Are there images that strike you? Close your eyes and listen to the passage again. See it play before your eyes. What do you see?

Smell. What do people smell in the passage? (bread and wine; the smell of mountain air; the stench of a dead or dying person) What smells are you reminded of as you read the passage? What smells can you relate to things in your life? (your mother's fresh baked bread; pine trees in the mountains; a nursing home)

Taste. What do people taste in the story? (bread or wine; their own sweat or blood; the taste of salty skin in a kiss) What tastes are you reminded of as you read the passage? What tastes can you relate to things in your life? (fresh bread; the taste in your mouth after being sick; a kiss to a child's feverish forehead)

5. The Hermeneutical Move

Hermeneutics is basically the practice of discovering and sharing what God's Word means to us today in our time, place, culture, and context. The hermeneutical move is asking the question "So what?" Discuss the following questions as a group:

- What is God's message to us today?
- What does this passage have to do with our lives? with the congregation's life? with the life of the community around us?
- What is so important about this passage?

F. Choosing a Focus

Supplies: newsprint, markers, tape

Invite participants to express the message of the Scripture in a word, phrase, or one sentence. As people begin to share their words, phrases, and sentences, write them on newsprint. In order for the group to get a sense of what everyone experienced and thought, keep this as a brainstorming session where all contributions are recorded on the newsprint. Post the newsprint on the wall.

Second, ask the group what is important to communicate about the Scripture. Perhaps it is the beauty of the words, the message itself, the power of the story experienced visually, or an incredible metaphor. Write these on newsprint as well and display on the wall.

Third, ask the group to take a moment to look at all the different newsprints posted on the wall. Then ask the group to begin to focus on what message they would like to present or what is important to communicate about the Scripture. It may quickly become clear or the group may have to work a little harder. However, it is important that the group make a decision of some sort. Remind the group that they may not be able to communicate everything about the Scripture (especially if the conversation has been rich, full, and diverse), but instead highlight a specific focus (especially if there are certain time limitations in worship to consider). After the group has chosen their focus, write it on a piece of newsprint and post it on the wall.

G. Choosing an Art Form

See H, activity 4 on p. 20.

H. Developing an Arts Piece for Worship

See H, activity 5 on p. 20.

I. Prepare and Rehearse

See I on p. 21–22.

J. Performing/Sharing

See J on p. 22.

K. Evaluate

See K on p. 22.

4

ENCOURAGING CREATIVITY

Introduction

The group working on arts and worship should, as a part of their regular routine together, participate in activities that stimulate creativity. As soon as a participant walks into the room, they should be greeted with something that gets them into the mindset of the subject at hand: liturgical art. As the group becomes more comfortable and experienced with the arts, the artistic choices they will be able to imagine and make for worship will become broader. Listed below are some great activities to help participants experience different artistic media and explore who they are as artists. You will also find many more activities listed in chapters 6 and 7.

Activities

Symbol of Self

Supplies: construction paper, markers, tape, scissors

Invite participants to use construction paper to cut out a symbol that represents themselves. It can be abstract or literal. Ask them to write their name on it and wear it as a name tag. Later, invite the group to share (in partners, small groups, or as one large group) their symbol and what it means.

Design a Stole

Supplies: copies of paper with a stole drawn on it (like a big upside down "U"), markers/crayons

Place the "stole papers" on tables with markers/crayons. Tape directions to the table, inviting participants to design their own stole. Draw one stole design as an example. Stoles can be designed around a certain subject, theme, or Bible verse, or you can just invite the participants to let their imaginations go.

Design a Tile

Supplies: wood or ceramic tiles, acrylic paints, paintbrushes, pencils, water, drop cloth (newsprint, newspaper, plastic, etc.)

Place the tiles on a table covered with a drop cloth. Invite participants to design their own tile. The tiles can be designed around a certain subject, theme, or Bible verse, or you can just invite them to let their imaginations go. Provide pencils for them to draw their design on the tile before they begin to paint.

Find a place to display the tiles. We have worked with congregations who have actually placed them on a wall in their youth room. You could also use them in a hallway or fellowship hall. For a portable display, attach them to a large piece of plywood.

Create a Mobile

Supplies: two sticks or dowels bound together in an X, string, a variety of art supplies (construction paper, glue, scissors, tape, yarn, fabric, glitter, markers, paint, crayons, etc.)

Hang the X from the ceiling using string. Place art materials on a nearby table. Tape directions on the table, inviting participants to create a symbol around a subject, theme, or Bible verse. Invite them to hang their symbol on the mobile. You may want to already have strings hung from the X so that they can easily attach their symbol to the mobile.

Shapes, Pictures, and Designs

Supplies: construction paper, cut in various shapes and sizes

Spread shapes on the table. Tape directions to the table, inviting participants to make a picture or design using the shapes. Participants can share with each other or guess what each picture is.

Comic Strips

Supplies: paper, markers/crayons, printed Bible story, tape

Spread paper and markers on table. Tape a Bible story on the table. If the story is a parable or short passage, you can simply use the text straight from the Bible. However, if the story is longer (for example, Jonah or Moses and Pharaoh), write a shorter synopsis. Tape directions to the table, inviting participants to make one frame telling a part of the story. Attach frames together to make the comic strip.

Coffee Filter Tie-dye

Supplies: tempera paint (either powder or diluted liquid paint), coffee filters, newspaper

This activity provides all the fun of tie-dying without a lot of the mess. Spread newspaper on a table. Fold a coffee filter in half over and over again until you have what looks like an ice-cream cone. Dip the corners of the folded filter in different colors of paint. The filter will draw the paint up into the filter. If you dampen the filter with water first, it will draw the paint faster and mix the colors more. After you are finished dipping, unfold the filter and let it dry on newspaper. You may want to designate an area where newspaper can be spread for drying the filters. You can leave the filter as it is or cut it into a shape (cross, heart, etc.) before or after dying it. Also, try folding it in different ways to see what color patterns can be formed.

Signing the Psalms

Supplies: paper with a psalm printed on it; sign language dictionary/book

Tape a psalm to the table. Tape directions to the table inviting people to learn the psalm in sign language by looking up certain highlighted words from the psalm. Another option is to photocopy the sign language symbols from a book and put them next to the appropriate words. *The Joy of Signing* by Lottie L. Riekehof (Springfield, MO: Gospel Publishing House, 1978) is helpful because it includes signs for Christian and theological words.

Musical Words

Supplies: a Scripture passage written on newsprint, a variety of children's musical instruments (tambourines, shakers, cymbals, sandpaper blocks, rhythm sticks, etc.)

In choosing a Scripture passage look for one that is full of imagery, emotional words, and contrast. Just about any psalm is good for this activity. Write the Scripture passage on a piece of newsprint and post it on the wall. As you write it, put spaces between each line or verse of the passage.

Gather a group around the newsprint. Ask them to each pick out a different musical instrument. Then invite them to choose one line of the Scripture passage where they think their instrument would serve as a good accompaniment. For example, if the line is about a rainstorm, someone might want to shake a tambourine lightly. If the line is about God's almighty power, someone might want to crash cymbals together. There is no right or wrong way to do this activity. Have fun with it! Experiment and enjoy.

After everyone has chosen a part of the Scripture, read the passage as people play their instruments when their line is read. Read the passage again, but this time have each participant read and play their part in turn. Read the passage a third time, but this time have the group read it in unison as they play their instruments in turn. Finally, do it again, but this time with instruments only. Listen to the sounds.

Same Tune, New Lyrics

Supplies: pens/pencils, paper, hymn books, songbooks

Place all the supplies on a table and ask the group to gather around the table. Ask the group to select a favorite hymn or song. After they have chosen their hymn, invite them to make up new lyrics to the tune. The lyrics can center around a certain subject, theme, or Bible verse, or you can just invite them to let their imaginations go. You may also do this activity as individuals. After the group is finished, make copies of the new lyrics and sing them together. Save the new lyrics to use at a future gathering or worship service.

5

Building A Group And Developing Trust

Introduction

When people in a group feel comfortable with each other and know each other, there is a greater likelihood that they will be successful. Individuals in groups that are working in arts and worship will often be asked to take risks by trying something new or expressing a side of themselves—the artist—in public that they do not know very well or did not even know was there. Therefore, it is essential that groups working on the arts engage in activities that help them get to know and trust one another. Besides the activities listed below, we suggest using *Silver Bullets* by Karl Rohnke (Dubuque, IA: Kendall/Hunt Publishing Company, 1984). You will also find helpful group-building activities that focus on storytelling in chapter 6.

Activities

Role Call

Ask participants to stand or raise their hands when the following items apply to them. This activity gives the participants a chance to see the demographics of the group.

- females/males
- socks/no socks
- prefer baths/prefer showers
- like country music/like rock 'n' roll/like classical

Continuum

Explain to the group that one side of the room is one extreme and the other side of the room is the other extreme. Indicate an imaginary line that goes from one end of the room to the other. Invite them to stand on the continuum line when you call out the two extremes. They can stand anywhere on that line depending on how they feel.

- mountain person or beach person
- gourmet food or fast food

- head in the clouds or realist
- organized or disorganized

Groupings

Invite the participants to gather in groups according to the categories you call out. Make sure that as you call out the categories, you point to a place in the room where each category group should go.

- fall, spring, winter, and summer birthdays
- lay people/clergy
- men/women
- break down by ages
- those wearing watches/those not wearing watches
- white socks/no socks/colored socks

Lines

This activity is adapted from *Silver Bullets* (see Resources, p. 85). Invite the participants to line up by certain categories, but with each line, give a limitation as to how they are able to communicate. You may want to start with easy ones where they are able to talk, then get more complicated.

- line up by birthday months (the group can talk to each other)
- line up by age (no talking)
- line up by eye color—darkest to lightest (no talking)
- line up by height (with eyes closed or blindfolded)

Name Aerobics

Invite participants to stand or sit in a circle. Instruct them to think of an action that they can do with their bodies that represents themselves (a characteristic, a hobby, etc.). Some examples are as follows: clapping, swinging a bat, kicking a ball, hopping, showing a big smile, and so forth.

After everyone has decided on an action, start the game by saying, "Hi, my name is _____" then do your action. The group then responds by saying, "Hi _____" and does your action. The person to the left goes next, saying his/her name and doing his/her action. The group repeats the name of the second person and does their action, then says your name and does your action. Keep going around the circle, repeating names and actions sequentially.

After you have completed the circle, ask everyone if they know one another's names. If you are wearing name tags, cover them up and let people test themselves. Tell the group that if they need to ask someone about their name, please do so. Ask if anyone in the group wants to volunteer to say everyone's names by memory. Invite everyone in the group to switch places in the circle, then go around doing everyone's names and signs again.

Musical Backs

Supplies: tape player, tape with short cuts of different kinds of music

Invite the group to form a circle and have them all face one direction. Tell the group that the person's back in front of them is now their canvas, on which they will interpret the music they hear. They might do small karate chops, deep massage on the shoulders, scratches, etc. Ask participants to tell their partners if they have any back trouble, so the game can be fun and not painful. Turn on the music and have fun!

Back-to-Back Dancing

Supplies: tape player, tape with short cuts of different kinds of music

Invite participants to each find a partner and turn back to back. Tell them to begin dancing when the music comes on. When the music switches, they must find a new partner and dance with them back to back until the music changes and they find another partner. If they can't find a partner at any time, tell them that "lost and found" will be at the front of the room, and it is there that they can find someone else who needs a partner.

Human Cameras

This activity is adapted from *Silver Bullets* (see Resources, p. 85). Invite participants to find a partner. Have the partners choose who will be the photographer and who will be the camera. Instruct the photographers that they are going to take their camera on a trust walk. The cameras should tell the photographers how they would like to be led (by the hand, with a hand on the elbow to steer, or by the shoulders being pushed from behind). Then the cameras should keep their eyes closed during their trust walk except as instructed below.

Tell the photographers that their job is to take very good care of the cameras by making sure they don't bump into anything or trip. Tell the photographers that they will take their camera to three different "picture sights." The pictures can be close-ups or big pictures. The idea is to be creative. When the camera's "head" is all lined up and ready for the picture, the photographer will press the camera's shoulder and the camera will open and close his/her eyes quickly like a shutter lens. After the photographer has taken the three pictures, the camera then "shows" the photographer what pictures he/she saw. This can be especially challenging depending on what pictures were taken. After they are finished, invite the partners to switch roles and do it again.

6

DRAMA

Introduction

The group you are working with has gone through a process of developing arts in worship. They have decided that they want to do a drama depicting a certain Scripture or theme. So, now what?

Your group could begin to search for material found in prepackaged drama books and scripts. However, often these resources can be limiting. It is hard to find drama that makes use of Reformed theology. It can also be difficult to find drama that goes beyond the superficial or common television situation comedy. So, where do you find the best drama?

If you can make the time and encourage your group to take on the task, the best drama is that which is the most meaningful and timely to the life of the congregation or the group whom you are serving. The resources for this kind of drama most often come not from professional scripts, but from the imaginations, thoughts, and ideas of the group.

Of course, what this means is that you now have to find people who write. How often have we heard, "I'm not a writer. I can't do that," or even worse, "I hate writing. I'm not going to do it!" Writing seems to conjure up images of red ink on white paper. It reminds people of their failures in English class or all-nighters sitting at a keyboard trying to write a research paper on something they could care less about. Because of bad experiences with writing, most people not only think they cannot write, but they will not write.

However, we are all storytellers. Everyone has told a story about this or that. Everyone has recounted a memory. Everyone has recounted a dream from the night before. Everyone has written a letter or a card. If you can tell a story, recount a memory or a dream, or write a letter, you can write drama.

We have also found that the best drama is the drama that not only comes out of the life of the people, but also paints a picture for the audience to ponder. The drama is the illustration to the written Word. The drama asks questions, inspires thought, encourages dialogue, but does not necessarily perform the function of the average television situation comedy or weekday drama. The most effective drama does not tie everything up in a nice package with a bow on top, but makes the audience think.

As Christians writing for the stage, our conviction is that the writer does not have the weighty responsibility of knowing all the right answers. The writer has the job of listening to God's Word, asking questions of it, and listening again for God's response.

Finally, the writer must choose how to best paint the picture for the congregation or group he/she is serving. What characters are appropriate? What do they say? What do they do? Where does the drama take the congregation? What's the beginning, middle, and end? Where is the climax?

Therefore, when you, as a leader, approach a novice writing group, let them know that they *can* write a drama. All it takes is imagination, a willingness to ask questions and listen for God's response, and a willingness to make choices.

In this chapter we will first look at some ways to warm up to writing. Then we will define three different forms of drama: Reader's Theater, monologues, and scenes. With each form of drama, you will find a process to begin writing. Finally, the chapter will end with some tips for effective casting and directing.

Warming Up to Writing

Some people are born with a special talent for writing, however, writing is also a skill that almost everyone can learn and develop. With a little imagination, one can create a story. With a little storytelling ability, one can write a script. Imagination, storytelling, and writing are a little like muscles in the body; they atrophy when they are not used. However, writing skills always have the potential to be built up, improved, and made stronger with use.

Make writing and storytelling a part of your regular gathering time—in fellowship gatherings, church school, worship, and study times. If writing and storytelling become a regular part of your time together, then it will not be as difficult to consider writing a drama.

As the group shares their writing, you, the leader, are provided the opportunity to identify the skills of the group. One may be great at starting a story, while another is excellent at creating the ending. One may be wonderful at generating ideas, while another is a good wordsmith. Be intentional about identifying these gifts to individuals and the group. Be diligent about encouraging them in their gifts. It will inspire them to do more.

The following are some games, exercises, and activities that build up imagination, storytelling, and writing.

Creating a Song Poem

Supplies: tape or CD player, copies of lyrics to a song you choose, pencils

Choose a song that is especially meaningful, popular, or works well with the theme or subject at hand. Give each person a copy of the lyrics to the song. Ask group members to circle words or phrases that speak to them or stand out to them as they listen to the song. After the song is over, have them write on the back of the paper a list of the words and phrases they circled. Then have them put each word into a phrase or sentence of their own that addresses the subject or theme the group is focusing on. When they are finished, they will have each created their own poem. You can ask the group to share in partners, threes, or with the whole group. It is helpful to offer the option of each individual choosing to share either the poem or only the words they circled.

Life Story in Thirty Seconds

Supplies: watch with a second hand

Invite group members to sit in a circle. If you have more than eight people, divide the group into smaller groups. Ask the group to decide who will go first (or you can decide who goes first using random criteria, such as who has the longest hair, oldest shoes, darkest eyes, etc.). Tell them that each person will have thirty seconds to tell their life story to the group. When you yell "Switch!" the person talking stops and the next person in the circle to the left immediately starts telling her/his life story. If someone is having trouble thinking of things to say, encourage the rest of the group to ask questions.

Highs and Lows

At each gathering, begin with the participants sharing their high and low during the week or during the time since you last were together. This encourages them to tell stories about their lives and make choices about what they will tell. Later, when you are writing a drama, ask what was the high or low of the character or situation. Identifying highs and lows with a character or situation can help the group choose or discover the beginning, end, or climax of their drama.

Add to the Poem

Supplies: large piece of paper, markers

Spread markers on a table around a large piece of paper. Write a couple of lines of your own to get the poem started. Tape directions on the table, inviting participants to add their own line to the poem.

Graffiti Wall

Supplies: newsprint, markers, tape

Draw a brick design on newsprint and post it on the wall. Invite people to respond in words, pictures, or designs to a certain subject (sin), theme

(Created to Create), or Bible passage ("we are all one body"). The graffiti wall can be used as an entering activity for one session or can be used for an entire series, workshop, or retreat.

Graffiti Sheets

Supplies: newsprint, markers, tape

Tape sheets of newsprint to tables or the walls. On each newsprint, write a statement for participants to respond to in any way that they like. (For example, Art is . . . ; When I think of artists, I . . . ; What I wish to get out of this workshop is . . . ; When I was sixteen, I thought God was . . . ; My favorite musical group when I was 25 was . . .) Be creative in your statements, making sure they address issues and needs of the group. The statements can be serious or fun and lighthearted.

Poetry Pieces

Supplies: Magnetic Poetry Kit (inquire at P.O. Box 14862, Minneapolis, MN 55414: kits for adults and children) or small pieces of construction paper with many different words on them (don't forget nouns, prepositions, adjectives, articles, adverbs, verbs, etc.)

Spread the words out on the table (or on a magnetic surface). Tape directions on the table, inviting participants to put the words together into their own poem.

Journaling

Supplies: set of journals (notebooks), construction paper, art supplies (markers, paint, crayons, magazines, stickers, glitter), glue, scissors, tape, pens/pencils

Place all of the supplies on the table and invite the participants to make their own personal journal by taking a notebook and gluing a piece of construction paper on the front. They may also use the construction paper to make a book cover (if the paper is large enough). Encourage them to decorate the front according to a theme, subject, passage, or they can just let their imagination go.

After everyone is finished, invite the group to make their first journal entry by writing down why they decorated the front as they did. Give participants five minutes. Tell them just to write what comes to mind. After five minutes, invite the group to share their journal covers with each other and explain them. Remind them that they only have to share as much as they want.

Use the journals in several different meeting times. If the group decides to leave the journals at their meeting place so they will not get lost or forgotten, make arrangements to keep them in a secure, confidential place. If the group decides to take their journals home, encourage a habit of bringing them to every meeting along with their Bibles.

The journals can be used for writing prayers; writing song poems (see pp. 38–39);

writing down questions about a certain Scripture passage; free writing (see below); or word association (see below).

A wonderful benefit of journaling is that a journal keeps a record of the writer's thoughts and feelings as he/she travels on his/her faith journey. The writer can also see her/his skill in writing improve as he/she looks back over what he/she has written. Journals are priceless records of time, thoughts, and ideas.

Free Writing

Free writing is a timed writing session where the writer simply puts the pen/pencil to the paper and records all ideas and thoughts that come into his/her head. Free writing is best done if it is given a theme/subject (identity, grace, forgiveness, etc.) or some sort of focus such as responding to a situation, story, or Scripture reading.

Word Association

In word association, the leader says a word and the writer writes down whatever word first comes into their mind. The leader may choose words that focus on a certain subject (words about faith, words about group dynamics, etc.). A variation on word association is to ask the writer to take his/her response words and put each one in a phrase or sentence. By doing this, the writer creates a poem.

Three Uses of Drama for the Stage

We will now explore three different ways to use drama on the stage: Reader's Theater, monologues, and scenes. We will define each and provide a hands-on process for creating a drama in each form. For examples and complete scripts in each of the three forms, see *Living in Community, Living in God, Living in the Light,* or *Living in the Real World* by Aimee Wallis Buchanan, Bill Buchanan, and Jodi B. Martin (Bedford, VA: Theological Expressions in Arts Ministry, 1998). These are compilations of scripts for youth that explore a variety of issues. For information and to order, contact T.E.A.M. at 1125 Fairfield Rd., Bedford, VA 24523.

Creating a Reader's Theater

Reader's Theater is a great starter for inexperienced writers of drama. It can be the easiest way to begin to write for the stage, yet it has the potential (as the writer develops his/her skill) to be as complex and intricate as desired.

Reader's Theater is a presentation of a drama or some other exposition with the actors usually speaking out to the audience instead of to one another. Reader's Theater is usually read from a script (thus the name). However, a Reader's Theater can be memorized and be played in a Greek Chorus style by adding liturgical movement to the spoken words.

Reader's Theater makes use of repetition of words, unison reading, reading over one another, echoing each other, and other effects like these. A Reader's Theater can be used to explore a theme or subject (such as baptism or the covenants God has made with us through history), to tell a story, or to present a Scripture passage.

Focus on the Subject or Theme

Remind the group of the chosen theme or subject that they will be writing about. It helps if you can put the theme into one word (love, justice, faith, etc.).

Brainstorm Synonyms

Ask the group to brainstorm different synonyms for the subject at hand. For example, if your topic is injustice, ask the group to brainstorm a list of words that are synonymous with injustice, such as "hate, dereliction, wrongdoing, unfairness." Write all responses on newsprint.

Brainstorm Definitions

Now ask the group to brainstorm definitions for the subject. Again with the example of "injustice," the group might say the "absence of justice, the violation of what is right," and so forth.

Brainstorm Examples

Now ask the group to brainstorm examples of the topic. Encourage the group to think of examples in three different subjects: global, biblical, and personal/communal (having to do with their own personal lives or their life as a group). For injustice, a global example would be the shooting of students in Tienanmen Square, Beijing, in 1989. A biblical example might be the tyranny of Pharaoh over the Israelites. A personal/communal example could be a statistic about rape or child abuse/neglect or a reference to something that has actually happened in the group's community and/or life.

Brainstorm a List of Questions

Ask the group to brainstorm a list of questions they have about the subject. If considering injustice, the group might ask the following: How do we stop it? What is God's intent for our world? Will injustice win in the end?

Organize

At this point, you may choose to begin to organize and write the Reader's Theater as a group or you may ask for a few volunteers to pull it together—especially if you have a very large group.

Think about the flow from beginning to middle to end. Ask yourself what you want the audience to think about as they leave. Then begin to organize your words, phrases, examples, and questions in a way that will help the audience explore the meaning of the subject.

Suggestions for Using Reader's Theater

- Reading Scripture in the Reader's Theater style with unison, parts, echo, and so on.
- To introduce and/or define a subject (e.g., God's covenants, justice, etc.)
- To read a play, story, or sermon to an audience
- To translate a Scripture reading into modern-day language (Have the modern-day language echo the Scripture reading.)

Creating Monologues

A monologue is performed by one person. That actor may speak directly to the audience or in soliloquy form, where they speak on stage but not directly to the audience. The monologue is great to use when you want to get into the inner psyche, motivations, and emotions of a character.

Choose the Character

Choose a character to focus on. The character may be biblical, historical, or modern, and may be real or fictional. Choose a character for whom the group has questions—someone whom the group would like to know better. Eagerness to know the character will provide inspiration for the work ahead.

Getting to Know the Character

It is not possible to write a monologue with integrity from the point of view of someone you do not know. So get to know the character by asking the following questions about the character and taking notes. Reflect on the notes with your group:

- What do we know about this person?
- What was she/he feeling?
- What was she/he thinking?
- What did she/he have to be concerned about?
- What was his/her history? life situation? cultural obligations?

What Is the Focus?

What is the message of the monologue? Do not write a ten-minute speech that rambles on from one thing to another, but do not write a first-person historical documentary answering all the above questions in vast detail either. Write a monologue where everything points to, leads to, or highlights the focus.

So, what is the focus? Here are some questions to help get you started. Use them to generate other questions and help you choose the focus. Unless you are doing a one man/woman show, you won't be able to answer all of them.

- Is the goal for the audience to experience some of this person's inner thoughts and feelings? to get to know them a little better?
- Is the goal to know this person's motivations for his/her actions?
- Is the goal to know the regrets of the character or the determination of the character?
- Is the goal to know the goals of the character?
- Is the goal to get the audience to relate to the character? to feel like they are the character?

Take Another Look

Take one more look at the character you have chosen. If you are doing a biblical character, ask yourself one more question: Considering the focus we have chosen, would it be helpful to do a monologue from a modern point of view based on this character? Often, if your goal is to get the audience to relate, it can be helpful to do two monologues: one from the biblical character and another from a modern parallel. A good example is the good Samaritan. Maybe the priest becomes a modern-day minister who sees an accident beside the road. Maybe the Samaritan is the outcast at school or work. The modern parallel is not always appropriate, nor always the best choice, but consider the possibility before making a decision.

Choose the Writer

At this point, the group needs to choose someone to do the writing. If more than one person wants to write, use the rest of the process in collaboration. It may be especially helpful, if you are doing a series of monologues, to give each person in the group a different character.

Freewriting

Now that the writer has background notes and is focused, they are ready to try freewriting in first person for five minutes. Start sentences with "I." Encourage writers to use their imagination and put themselves in the character's shoes. Tell them to let go and record whatever comes to mind.

After five minutes, stop and check in: Have they drawn a blank? Are they ready to write more? If they are ready to write more, then let them do so. Keep writing and remind them to keep the focus of the monologue in mind.

If some are drawing a blank, then back up. Go slow. Encourage them to look at their notes. Ask them to close their eyes and picture the character speaking to them. What is she or he saying? What is she or he feeling or thinking? Write it down. If some are still drawing a blank, take a break. Then ask each person to share some of their ideas with a partner. Sometimes sharing ideas out loud or listening to the ideas of others can spur on thoughts. Whatever you do, don't give up! It is possible to do this with great results.

Editing

Once the group has finished freewriting, it is time to go back and do some fine-tuning. Make it a policy to never accept a first draft as the final draft. Here are some things to look for:

- Make the first sentence count for something. It should draw the audience in.
- Make the monologue have a beginning and an end, with a climax somewhere in between. A monologue should not just be a creative rambling, but should lead the audience somewhere. For the writer, the task is to lead the audience to the chosen focus.
- Read it out loud. Does it sound like how the character would talk and not how they would write? People often do not talk in complete sentences, but are more likely to use run-ons and fragments (For example, He dissed me—stepped all over me. I felt like . . . he wouldn't pay attention to me.) However, some characters would speak quite formally (For example, He ignored me and crushed my soul. I felt rejected and lost. He would not pay attention to me.)
- Make the last sentence count for something. Just as you grabbed the audience at the beginning, grab them at the end.

Suggestions for Using Monologues

- Play biblical characters: Do one monologue by one biblical character, or do several monologues by several characters who appear in a common scene (the three women at the empty tomb).
- Play modern characters all reacting to the same thing (a series of characters explaining the motivation to come to church).
- Play modern characters that mirror biblical characters (the woman caught in adultery becomes a pregnant teenager).

Creating Scenes

A scene is a short story or vignette told through the dialogue and action of characters. Scenes are excellent to use when you want to dramatize a subject. A series of scenes can be used to explore a certain theme or subject from different angles (for example, several scenes depicting faith in everyday life).

A series of scenes can also be combined to make a full length play. For our purposes, we will be concentrating on the short scene for use in worship or any thematic presentation.

As the group plans, develops, and write the scenes, encourage them to stay away from moralistic endings and singsong wrap-ups. Reject the idea of "skits" that give a simple message and leave the audience with little to really think about. The purpose of the scene is to get the audience to think about their lives and faith. Jesus did this with his parables. The scene should leave the audience in a state of questioning who they are, a state of awe about who God is, and the gift of motivation to continue working on their faith.

Choose the Focus

Choose your theme or Scripture passage and the focus or goal of the scene. Ask the following questions:

- Is the goal to portray the story of a Scripture passage?
- Is the goal to show a modern version of a Scripture passage?
- Is the goal to show the significance of a certain theme? (forgiveness, trust, and so on)
- Is the goal to show how faith is relevant to real life situations?
- Is the goal to expound on what could have or might have happened before or after some biblical scene?
- Is the goal to introduce a certain theme?

Keep asking questions until the group has defined the focus of the drama scene(s).

Also, ask these very important questions:

- Who is your audience? Ask this question in order to have a frame of reference as you begin to make decisions. If the group is doing a scene as a part of the proclamation for an intergenerational worship, then appropriating a scene from Saturday Night Live may not be your best option.
- Who is available to act? What does the space where you will perform look like? What are its limitations and possibilities? How much time do you have before you need to be ready? Answering these very important practical questions now will eliminate unneeded complications later. However, see the answers to these questions as simply pieces of the puzzle, not finite limits that cannot be overcome. It would be a shame for an amazing idea to be overlooked because of a logistical limitation without first thinking creatively about both the idea and the logistical limitation.

Outline the Scene

It is important to outline the scene in order to provide a road map for the dialogue. The writer must know where he/she is beginning and where he/she is trying to end up.

If you are using a biblical story or adapting a story, you will have some choices to make that will be different from choices you will make if writing an original scene. Let's look at them separately.

Adapting a Story. In outlining a biblical story or adapting a story, most of the work has been done for you because the story has already been written. Before you begin making choices, though, remember that Scripture has a life of its own and it is not our word, but God's Word. Thus we must make choices with integrity and a background of study and respect toward the passage. God does not wish for us to paste our own meaning over Scripture, but to look for meaning within the Scripture—to listen for the Holy Spirit bringing new life to us through God's Word. God does invite us to be creative and to spread God's Word throughout the world, but let us always remember whose Word it is.

Your choices begin with selecting the dialogue, dealing with narration, and choosing what part of the story you will highlight.

In selecting dialogue, you must choose what style you will write in: biblical style, modern language, or something in between. Consider what would be most appropriate for your purposes.

In dealing with narration, you will need to decide how to set up the story for the audience so that it makes sense. In prose writing, this is done through description of the scene and characters. Will you choose to have a narrator to introduce the scene? Will you choose to "narrate" the scene through dialogue, set design, or a note in the bulletin/program?

You will need to make decisions as to what you will highlight in the story. If your goal is to show how the story is relevant to life or to show how it supports a certain theme, you will need to make some choices in how the story is told so that it highlights what you chose. This can be done through a pause, the way the scene is acted or played, or by the way the dialogue is written.

Outlining an Original Scene. When writing an original scene, outlining will be more difficult because it is not already provided for you. It may be helpful at this time for the group to do some role playing. The following are two different approaches to the role play. As each role play is done, make sure those in the audience have pen and paper and invite them to write down any notes or specific lines that they really liked. In a role play situation, the idea can come and go so quickly that the group is left thinking, "Now what was that I really liked?" or, "Oh! I loved that line she said. What was it?" And chances are no one will remember.

1. General Role Play. Divide your group into threes or pairs. The small groups can be bigger or smaller depending on the size of your group. Give all the groups the general theme (conflict, faith, trust, etc.). Tell each group they have fifteen minutes to choose a scenario, practice it, and make plans for presenting it. Their scene should have specific characters and a beginning, middle, and end.

Invite each group to act out their scene in front of the other groups. If your group has never done this before, they may want more time. However, stress that the importance of the activity is not to create a complete and ready scene, but to get ideas. The polishing will come later.

Note: If your group members are not ready or are very uncomfortable with the idea of acting in front of each other, invite them to create an outline of their scene (with specific characters and a beginning, middle, and end) and share the outline with the group.

2. Tag-team Role Play. Invite the group to choose a specific scenario with specific characters. (If you are trying to write more than one scene, split your group into threes or pairs and ask each group to choose so you get a list of different scenarios.) For example, if the theme was conflict, then the group would need to identify the basic conflict and the characters. When choosing the characters, give them names and some background. For example, the group might say: The conflict is over grades at school. The characters are Lucy, the underachieving student; her mother, the overachieving company executive; and Joey, the bratty little brother.

Ask for volunteers to play the characters. Tell the group that this is a tag-team role play where the original volunteers for the parts can be replaced by anyone in the group. All a person has to do is walk into the scene and touch the shoulder of the person whose character they now want to play. The first actor will then exit the scene while the scene continues with the new actor. There should be no breaks. Everything should keep going as if nothing happened.

Invite the original volunteers to begin the scene when they are ready. If they are really nervous or resistant, give them a few minutes to do some planning. You may repeat this process with several different scenarios.

This type of role playing is especially helpful because the whole group actively participates in the role play. Everyone is invested. It also gives novice or timid role players a safety net. If they can't think of anything, then someone can come in to relieve them.

The most important part of role playing is to have fun with it. Role playing should not be turned into an improvisation or acting test, but should be something that gets the creative juices flowing. It is a way to see what is important to the group about a subject or theme. It is an opportunity to see how our faith is enacted in our life stories. It is a time for the group to support each other and encourage creativity in each other.

After the role plays, energy will have been created around the subject. Specific ideas will have emerged. Now the group can make some choices. As a debriefing to the role plays, discuss the following questions:

- List all the scenes that were done from beginning to end. Remember characters, situations, and what happened.
- What were you feeling when it was your turn to do a role play? What were you thinking?
- Which did you like better: watching or acting? Why?
- What did you like about the role plays themselves?
- What were the common threads between the scenes?
- What scenes would we like to expand on for our presentation?

Choosing Characters

After the group has decided what specific scenes they are going to outline, they will need to choose specific characters. Again, if you are portraying a biblical story, this will be easier than if you are writing an original scene. In selecting a group of characters, think about the following:

- The fewer the characters, the easier it is to write.
- The characters should be relevant to the story.
- Don't add a character to your script unless the character contributes to the goal and the telling of the story.
- The characters should be realistic or within the boundaries of your story. This doesn't mean that you cannot use mythical characters. The Ghost of Christmas Past is relevant to the story of Ebenezer Scrooge in *A Christmas Carol* even if the ghost is not a realistic part of everyday life.
- Each character should have a specific motivation or "I want." The "I want" of a character motivates them to act a certain way, say certain things, and alienate or align with certain other characters or ideas. The "I want" of one character may be to have everything his/her way, while the "I want" of another character may be just to get out of the scene because they have better things to do with their time and really don't care about what is going on. Identifying the "I want" of each character is critical because it will help the writer keep the character's actions and words consistent, which will give the character a clear identity. If your group is confused about the "I want" concept, play the following game.

The "I Want" Game

Supplies: a specific scenario, "I want" sheets

Ask for volunteers to participate in a role play that you have brought. Tell the group that the object of the game is to figure out the "I wants" or motivations of the role players. Explain what an "I want" is by referring to the previous definition.

Ask the volunteers to stand in front of the group. Tell them the situation they will be role playing. You may choose to bring to the group whatever you think is relevant or simple for them to play (for example, a discussion about what to do with $20,000 that has been given to the church and designated to use for some sort of building project).

Give each volunteer a sheet of paper that has an "I want" on it. Instruct them to not show it to anyone, but only look at it themselves. They are to keep their "I want" a secret. Some ideas are as follows: I just want to get out of here. I'm sleepy. I want whatever the person to my left wants. I want my way and that's it. I want there to be peace and unity. I want to eat. I want anything except what she/he (*designate a name*) wants. I want no one to notice me.

After everyone has their "I want," the role play may begin. After three to four minutes, stop the action. Ask the audience if they know who is who. If they need more time, keep going until all the "I wants" have been discovered.

Writing

Once the group has chosen characters, a scene, and written an outline, it is time to write. At this point, the group may decide how to divide writing tasks.

As each person begins writing, remind them of the following:

- A scene should have a beginning, a middle, and an end. Somewhere in between, there should be some kind of climax.
- Be consistent. Each character's "I want," way of speaking, alienations, and alignments should be consistent throughout the whole scene unless there is a reason for it to change.
- In writing dialogue, lines should be kept short. When people are inconversation, they usually talk in short quips to each other, exchanging back and forth. People do not speak in paragraphs to each other unless they are telling a story, have a purpose to talk awhile, or it is in their personality to talk in long waves.
- Also, people do not necessarily talk in complete sentences.

Editing

Once you have finished the first draft, it is time to go back and do some fine-tuning. *Remember:* Make it a policy to never accept a first draft as the final draft. Do the following steps:

1. Review the goal of the scene. Does the scene reflect the goal both in the dialogue and in the action of the characters?

2. Review the outline. Does the scene follow the outline? Does it have a beginning, a middle, and an end? Or did the scene end up going in a different direction? Maybe you discovered something new in the writing and the new ending is even better. Or maybe you rambled off and forgot the designated pathway.

3. Review the "I wants" of the character. Are the characters consistent? If they change, do they change for a reason?

4. Read the scene out loud. You may read alone or have a group read the different parts in order to hear different voices for the different characters. Is there any word or dialogue that needs changing? Does it sound like how "real people" talk?

5. Finally, revise the scene. Know also that after the scene has been cast and you begin to stage it, you may discover other changes that seem appropriate. Actors, directors, and onlookers may see something that you did not. Sometimes a scene that looks great on paper or even when read out loud just does not play well on stage. Be open to these changes, knowing that you have created a living, breathing document that will continue to grow as you and others work with it.

Suggestions for Using Scenes

- Enact the Scripture.
- Play the characters of the biblical story as a continuation of the action that took place in the Scripture reading.
- Play modern characters in a parallel story to the Scripture or as a continuation of the action that took place in the Scripture reading.
- Adapt popular "scenes" from today's media (game shows, TV sitcoms and dramas, commercials, radio programs, and so on).
- Play modern characters and biblical characters talking to each other.

Mixing Drama Media

By using more than one form of drama, you can often portray more than if restricted to a certain genre. The following is one example of thinking about drama in a multimedia format.

Imagine starting with a biblical portrayal of the good Samaritan. Actors enter in period costume and do a drama depicting the story. Next the actors remove their costumes on stage as they cross back to their entrance points. They portray the good Samaritan story again, but this time through modern characters. Next each modern character does a monologue that emphasizes their point of view. After the monologues, the modern characters cross to each other and begin to talk in a scene that emphasizes forgiveness and faith.

By using the multimedia format, the drama portrayed the good Samaritan story in two ways (biblical and modern). The monologues allow the character's inner thoughts, feelings, and motivations to be revealed. The scene depicts what might have happened if the characters had gathered together, talked, and perhaps been transformed by God's forgiveness and a new faith. Each drama media helps to meet a certain goal—whether it's portraying the story, getting in the mind of a character, or imagining what could have happened later. Each media has become a part of a greater whole.

Of course, there is such a thing as "biting off more than you can chew." If your group is just beginning this process, have them use their enthusiasm and energy to achieve a very focused and attainable goal, such as a short monologue, Reader's Theater, or a scene that portrays a biblical story. Then, as they grow in confidence and skill, they can begin to broaden.

Notes to the Director

The director is the person who is responsible for the big picture and how the small details contribute to the big picture. The director oversees all the activities that go on in presenting a drama, from the actual staging to technical issues to publicity.

The director is the person who is responsible for the staging of a drama. The director blocks the drama; that is, puts it on stage and tells people where to stand and move on stage. The director, usually with some help from skilled people, makes decisions about set designs, lighting, sound, and any other technical issues. The director is also the acting coach for the actors.

The director's greatest responsibility is setting the tone from the first rehearsal through the final presentation of the drama. The director is a minister to those with whom he/she works, and the director helps them minister to each other. Again and again, our experience has been that ministry takes place through the process of creating, as well as the end result. In working together to minister through the arts to a group of people, we experience faith, love, hope, and trust. The director sets the tone with his or her leadership style, working habits, and faith life.

Casting

One of the great things about theater is that there is usually a job for everyone. Not everyone may want to act, but they can find a place somewhere else in costuming, set design and production, programming, lights, sound, publicity, backdrops, or mechanics. Anyone who wants to be involved can find a place that uses their gifts. However, of all the opportunities for people in theater, the cast list can create the most tension and conflict. There are ways to deal with casting that are both productive and faithful.

There are many ways to cast without having to audition. Because we are Christian, we want to uphold ministry and not competition. We want to affirm all participants and not make distinctions between winners and losers. We want to identify the gifts of everyone and not just those who make the cast list.

By being a creative problem solver, the director can figure out how to use all who want to be involved. Sometimes, by simply gathering the group together and asking for volunteers for the different parts, everyone ends up getting a part and is happy. Sometimes people want the same part and often will work it out themselves. However, sometimes you, as the director, may need to give a little guidance. Have them look at each other's gifts. Who fits the role better? Have them look at what they are doing in other parts of the presentation. Maybe one already has a part elsewhere in the program or perhaps they would like to switch that part for the one at hand.

After you get to know your group and as the group begins to work together, you will be able to identify the gifts and strengths of those in the group. Often after having worked with a group for a while, we will precast the roles. Then, as a group, we will go over the cast list to see if it looks okay to them. We point out why we gave the parts to whom. It is not a matter of who is better than who, but who fits each role. The role and actor are like two puzzle pieces that lock together. Also, we explain that decisions must be made by logistics, by the needs for playing the character, by the abilities of each person, and by the way the Holy Spirit guides.

Sometimes it is just not clear who should play what part. Often the group can make difficult decisions about casting by reading the scene or a part of the scene several times with different people reading the parts. After a few readings, the group can see who seems to fit each role.

Directing the Drama

Again, as a director, your most important job is ministry. And one of the ways a director can minister faithfully and effectively is to identify gifts. It is your job to see the gifts of each person in the scene and it is your job to help the actor identify and cultivate those gifts. Someone may be weak on vocal projection, but excellent with their facial expressions. It is your responsibility, as director, to balance your pleas for the person to speak up with compliments on their facial expressions. We have repeatedly found that the person who understands and can affirm their own gifts is much more likely to listen and want to improve on their growing points.

As a director, not only are you there to encourage the actors as individuals, but also to encourage the group as an ensemble. The two most important things for the group to work toward as an ensemble are focus and energy. If each person keeps their complete attention focused on the task and each person directs their energy toward the group, the scene will play beautifully. However, if one person drifts, then he/she takes the whole scene down with him/her. In any athletic team, band, or choir, all the players must do their part. If one person loses focus or lacks energy, the chord sung or played will sound terrible, and the play practiced over and over will be ineffective. However, if everyone is focused and giving all their energy, no chord ever sounded more beautiful and no team was ever more competent in executing plays. It is no different with ensemble acting.

Focusing and Warm-up Activities

Every time the drama group gathers for rehearsal and/or performance, it is important that they warm up. Just as no football player would play without doing his stretches first and no opera singer would go on stage without doing her scales first, the drama group's warm-up is just as important.

Warm-ups should take place where distractions can be kept to a minimum. They should be done standing in a circle with all the focus and energy going to the middle of the circle. It is helpful to build a routine that is consistent and familiar. That way the group can focus more on the desired effects of the warm-up instead of how exactly to do it. Your warm-up time should take no more than fifteen minutes. Any more and the warm-up becomes an exercise in tiring out instead of warming up! We want to prime the pumps, not drain them.

If you are rehearsing, do your warm-up immediately before you hit the stage. Do not warm up then sit down to talk about costumes. This defeats the purpose. Take care of business before warm-ups or after the rehearsal.

If you are performing, have actors put on costumes and makeup, then warm up. If warm-ups must be done before putting on costumes and makeup, because of costume considerations, then do a mini warm-up right before the actual performance. However, finish any warm-up about ten minutes prior to the performance simply so actors can have some quiet time to get their minds on their places, their lines, and the rest of the performance.

The following are some great warm-ups we have used over the years. You may pick and choose or follow each exercise in the order given for a process of warming up. Regardless, we do recommend warming up body, face, and voice, and focus in that order. Spiritual warm-ups may take place at the beginning or end depending on your group's preference.

Body

Taking Neutral. After everyone has taken their place in the circle, ask them to stand in neutral: feet shoulder length apart, hands at side, shoulders relaxed, and standing straight up. Tell them that whenever they do any warm-ups, unless otherwise instructed, this is how they should stand.

Make a habit of also standing in neutral on stage. It gets rid of little dances, swaying, and hand fidgeting that people do on stage when they don't know what else to do or are just plain nervous.

Note: Look for more body warm-ups on pp. 62–64.

Shake Down. Invite the group to shake one hand, then the other. Shake their hips next. Then one foot. Then the other foot. Tell them they will shake each hand, hip, and foot for a count of 5, then 4, then 3, 2, and 1. Everyone will count together and count loud (using projection). At the end, everyone should shake all over and yell loudly. This is fun and the pace should be quick but manageable.

Up to the Sky/Down to the Ground. Ask the group to breathe in deeply and slowly through their nose and out through their mouth. Repeat a couple of times. Now invite the group to raise their arms when they inhale and lower them when they exhale. Repeat a couple of times. Ask the group when they inhale to raise their arms and stretch up to the sky by raising up on their toes, then when they exhale, to lower their arms and come back down to feet flat on the ground. Repeat a couple of times.

Ask the participants to repeat the exercise, except when they exhale, their hands should go all the way down to the ground by bending at the waist and hanging. The object is not to touch the ground with legs straight, but to simply hang at the waist comfortably, bending knees if need be. Swing from side to side. Nod your head "yes," then shake your head "no." Then, ask them to slowly raise up, straightening one vertebrae at a time. (This is a good stretch, plus it helps prevent head rushes!) As they raise up, tell them to roll their shoulders back, then forward. Look over their right shoulders. Look over their left shoulders. Look down. Then ask them to stretch out anything else that feels like it needs stretching.

Face and Voice

Taking Neutral. In all the voice and facial warm-ups, it is important to watch that people stay in neutral. Discourage people from pushing their neck forward or scrunching up their shoulders. This tenses the muscles they are trying to relax and warm up.

Chewing Gum. Ask the group to stand in a circle. Invite them to pretend that they are chewing the biggest piece of bubble gum they have ever imagined. They should chew with their mouths open, stretching the jaw as far wide as they can. It is fun to make the chewing noises as you do this.

Little Face/Big Face. Invite the group to first make the tiniest faces they can possibly make by scrunching their eyes together, pushing their lips together, and squeezing every muscle in their face in and to the center. They can also make little squeaky mouse noises while they do it. Then ask them to make the biggest faces they can possibly make by opening their eyes and mouths wide, eyebrows up. Push the facial muscles out and away from the center. They can roar like lions when they do this. Repeat a few times.

Tongue-Twister Chants. Each time the group chants a tongue twister, they are not only warming up their mouth and tongue so they are less likely to stumble over words later, but they are also practicing projection. Therefore, each tongue-twister chant should start by breathing in deeply through the nose and then speaking loudly by pushing from the diaphragm (not the throat). Anyone who projects from the throat will risk losing their voice and possibly even damaging their vocal chords. It may be helpful to have a choir director or a singer come in and teach your group about projection.

Ask the group to chant with you in the rhythm of your clap, "Red leather. Yellow leather." Increase the rhythm as the chant continues.

The following tongue-twister chants can also be used:

- Unique New York
- Whether the weather is cold, whether the weather is hot, we'll be together whatever the weather, whether we like it or not.
- Rubber baby buggy bumpers
- Hey batter, batter, batter! Swing batter, batter, batter. He (or she) can't hit. He can't hit. He can't hit.

Focus and Energy

Zing. The purpose of "Zing" is to develop concentration, create energy, and get a group to work together. Invite the group to get in a circle, standing about a foot apart from people on either side of them. Tell them to put their hands together like praying hands and then point them toward the center of the circle. Their hands are their zingers. One person starts the game by zinging (pointing and thrusting your zinger out to someone else in the group) someone else in the group while loudly saying, "Zing!" The object is not to trick anyone, but to be clear about who you are zinging. As soon as a person is zinged, they can either zing back the same person or zing someone else. The object is to see how fast the group can pass the zing. It is helpful to stop after a while (especially if the group gets confused or tired). Instruct everyone to take a deep breath, shake out their hands, and then start again.

Coach's Talk. While the group is still standing in the circle, take the time to give a coach's talk. If you are getting ready to rehearse, remind them of the specific focus of the rehearsal, highlight what they are doing well, and identify any areas they need to work on. If you are getting ready to perform, remind the group of how hard they worked, how God is with them always, and how much you appreciate them. A little encouragement from the leader can go a long way.

Spiritual

A spiritual warm-up is just as important as any of the above warm-up activities. If we are writing, working, acting, and rehearsing in order to portray and express God's word and message, then we must make sure we are connected with the one who is the subject of our work. We must thank God, seek God's will, and ask God for energy to do the work God has set before us.

As a group, decide whether you will do the spiritual warm-up at the beginning or end of your warm-up. You may decide to do it at both times (begin with a prayer and end by singing a song).

Some options for spiritual warm-ups include the following:

- singing a familiar song
- praying a prayer (either in unison, around the circle, or one person leading)
- breathing deeply and silently, focusing on God
- reciting Scripture (The group could choose to add movement to it.)

Evaluating

Before moving to the next drama piece or task, make sure the group has time to evaluate the process, the performance, and the congregation's reaction. It is important that the group learn and grow from each experience they have together. Discuss the following questions:

- What did we do well during the performance? What could we have done better?
- What did we communicate?
- What did the congregation feel/think?
- What did we feel/think?
- What went well at work times and rehearsals? What could we have done better?
- How was the process of developing the drama?
- What should we keep doing?
- What do we want to do next?

7

LITURGICAL MOVEMENT

Introduction

Liturgical movement happens every Sunday in every church. Many people might object and say, "We have never had dancing in our church." However, liturgical movement is not only dance. It is the movement occurring during liturgy. It is simply any movement done in response to God's Word or God's action in our lives. Liturgical movement happens when we rise to sing a hymn or reach out to greet our neighbor. It happens as we bow our heads to pray or as the preacher gestures and moves during her/his sermon. Our gestures and body language communicate the wide spectrum of emotions we feel and the concepts we ponder. Liturgical movement happens in our movements both intentional and unintentional, conscious and unconscious. The next time you participate in a worship service, note the ebb and flow of movement during liturgy.

This chapter is written to help those who want to build on and expand opportunities for members of their congregation to experience liturgical movement. The chapter suggests ways to make liturgical movement an intentional practice of worshiping God. Included are instructions describing how to gather a group together and get them to do liturgical movement. It also gives a process that aids a group in choreographing and creating an actual movement piece.

Why Do Liturgical Movement?

People learn and comprehend differently. Some people learn by listening, many by watching, and there are still others who need to experience something before they can understand it. Others may learn through a combination of listening and seeing or doing and watching. Liturgical movement can be another avenue for people to experience God's Word and is especially helpful to visual learners. It can enhance Scripture by bringing the words of Scripture to life. It can make abstract concepts such as salvation and grace become more concrete. A workshop participant once told us that liturgical movement brings the story alive and puts her there in the moment. By watching the movements and emotions of the dancers, it helps her understand more clearly the meaning of the Scripture.

Churches are called to "make disciples of all nations, baptizing them in the name of the Father and of the Son and of the Holy Spirit, and teaching them to obey everything that [Jesus has] commanded . . ." (Matt. 28:19). Liturgical movement provides a method for the church to answer that call by using an important and new method to reach visual learners and to teach God's ways, God's Word, and God's grace.

People also express themselves in numerous ways. The spoken and written word are the most common ways people communicate how they feel or what they think. Some people find it easier to express themselves through singing, and still others use the language of the body. They are not content to say, "I love you, Lord," without raising their arms and reaching their hands toward the sky. Churches are called to provide opportunities that enable all people to follow Jesus' commandment, "Love the Lord your God with all your heart, and with all your soul, and with all your mind" (Matt. 22:37). Liturgical movement provides an opportunity for those who are oriented to more active, physical expressions of their love for God to lead and participate in worship.

Introducing Liturgical Movement to Your Church

If the use of liturgical movement in worship excites you or if this chapter revives your creative energy so that you want to start choreographing pieces for worship today, that is wonderful! However, a note of caution before we get started.

Ask yourself or the group with whom you will be working to first evaluate your congregation. Find out what members think or how they feel about liturgical movement. Before you make a request to the worship committee, research what reactions might occur if a liturgical movement piece was used during worship.

Liturgical movement can be very threatening to people. It is often seen as not proper or going against the traditional form of worship. Because liturgical movement involves touching, it can stir up many uncomfortable emotions. Liturgical movement is an intimate way of relating to one another. It can be very intimidating just for two people to stand next to one another. It can be even more disturbing for someone to watch two people move together.

Ask yourself or the group that is planning arts in worship the following questions:

• What is the congregation ready for?

- Is the congregation responsive to drama or other creative elements in worship?
- How do they usually react to something different or unusual in worship?
- What steps should we take in order to be at a place where liturgical movement would be an acceptable form of worship?

If your congregation has not experienced any type of creative art element in worship previously, it will be difficult to answer the above questions. However, you can test the mood and atmosphere of your congregation. Observe the congregation during the Passing of the Peace, morning welcome, or as people enter the sanctuary and take their seats. Do people readily turn to their neighbor and speak? Or do they stiffly shake the hand of the person next to them and then sit down? The less comfortable they are with this element of worship, the less likely they are going to be responsive to a liturgical movement piece performed during a worship service. Make performing a liturgical movement piece in a worship service your goal. Then back up and slowly begin to integrate liturgical movement into the worship service in new ways.

Liturgical movement can be introduced in a variety of ways. The important thing to remember is to introduce liturgical movement slowly until it becomes an integral part of worship. The following are just a few ways liturgical movement can be introduced to a congregation.

Children's Sermons
- Do a liturgical movement piece for the Bible story reading to the children.
- Children can wave streamers or do other movements in response to a certain word that is said or song they sing.

Choir
- Ask the choir to add gestures or movements to an anthem.
- Enter from different places in the sanctuary for a processional hymn.

Liturgy
- People can hold hands or raise up their arms during a prayer.
- Movements can be added to a Call to Worship, a prayer of confession, or an affirmation of faith. The congregation can participate by following a person who is demonstrating the movements while the liturgy is read.

Retreats
- Teach participants actions to a favorite hymn or song.

- Perform a liturgical movement piece during a worship service or keynote in the more casual atmosphere of a retreat.

Getting Started

Gathering a Group

The group that gathers will be responsible for the development of the movement piece. They will create the movements, choose the type of accompaniment, and work out all of the logistical aspects of performing a piece. It is not necessary for all participants to actually perform the piece. It is important for there to be a variety of perspectives giving input into the production.

The group may be the same group that went through the experiential or deductive process for developing arts in worship. Another possibility is for a few members of that original group to ask other people in the congregation to work on a liturgical movement piece. As you gather the group, think again about where and for whom you are planning on having the piece performed. Gather a group of people who are a representative mix of those who will be watching the liturgical movement. Ask for volunteers and recruit those people who have shown an interest in creative worship elements.

A good size for a liturgical movement group is six to eight people. A group of this size allows for many combinations and arrangements of people. If you have more people who are interested in participating, it is always possible to divide up and work on separate sections. Just remember that the more people involved, the harder it is to choreograph. It can also become confusing for the congregation to try to watch a large number of people performing, especially if they are new to watching liturgical movement.

Finding a Space

Find a space in the church where the group can move freely. Start in a classroom where tables and chairs have been removed. When the liturgical movement piece is complete, rehearse it in the space where you will be performing.

Selecting a Passage

If the group has gone through the experiential or deductive process described earlier in the workbook, then a passage will have already been selected. If not, select a theme or Scripture passage that has been chosen for the service in which the piece will be performed. If the group has not secured a time to actually perform in worship, but is gathering to simply get familiar with liturgical movement, pick a passage full of vivid words and rich with action verbs. These passages are especially helpful to novice liturgical movers as they seek to turn words into movements.

Before you begin the actual choreography, the group will need to have studied the passage. We highly recommend using the experiential or deductive process presented earlier in the workbook. At the very least, see chapter 3 for guidance on the exegesis of a Scripture passage (pp. 26–27) . It is imperative that you search out the meaning of the passage—God's purpose for us in the reading of the Word—before you begin to choreograph.

We once led a group of youth who were using Eph. 4:1–4 as a theme for a retreat. In the New International Version, the passage begins, "As a prisoner for the Lord." The youth identified with Paul's prisoner image. They saw themselves as prisoners. They wanted to focus on all that imprisoned them "just like Paul did." Because we had done research and were clear about Paul's message, we were able to communicate to them that Paul was simply referring to the fact that he was writing the letter in prison and not necessarily using prison as a metaphor for Christians.

Getting a Group to Move

Warming Up

Every time the liturgical movement group gathers for rehearsal and/or performance, it is important that they warm up. Liturgical movement requires people to bend and stretch in ways that may not be a part of their everyday routine. It is important to warm up the body before you begin any of the activities. Warm-ups are designed to get the blood flowing to all parts of the body and to get the heart pumping above its resting rate.

Schedule warm-ups in a place where there are no distractions or where distractions can be kept to a minimum. They should be done standing in a circle, with all the focus and energy going to the middle of the circle. It is helpful to build a routine that is consistent and familiar. That way the group can focus more on the desired effects of the warm-up instead of how exactly to do it. Your warm-up time should take no more than fifteen minutes. Any more and the warm-up becomes an exercise in tiring out instead of warming up!

If you are rehearsing, do your warm-up immediately before you hit the stage. Do not warm up then sit down to talk about costumes. This defeats the purpose. Conduct business before warm-ups or after the rehearsal.

If you are performing, have actors put on costumes and makeup, then warm up. If warm-ups must be done before putting on costumes and makeup because of costume considerations, then do a mini warm-up right before the actual performance. However, finish any warm-up about ten minutes prior to performance simply so the movers can have some quiet time to get their minds on their performance.

The following are some great, fun, and easy warm-ups we have used over the years. If your group is meeting on a regular basis, you may want to develop a consistent warm-up routine. You or others in the group may have other ideas for movement warm-ups. Just remember to always involve the whole body. You will also find more warm-up ideas in chapter 6.

Make sure you include time for the participants to warm up spiritually. Spiritual warm-ups allow people a quiet moment to focus, ask God for guidance, and remember that God is in control of the work at hand. Spiritual warm-ups can be a movement prayer, deep breathing, a song, or a moment of silence. You can find other spiritual warm-up ideas in chapter 6 (p. 57).

Name Aerobics. Invite the group to stand or sit in a circle. Instruct them to think of an action that they can do with their bodies that represents themselves (a characteristic, a hobby, etc.). Some examples are clapping, swinging a bat, kicking a ball, hopping, showing a big smile, and soon.

After everyone has decided on an action, start the game by saying, "Hi, my name is _____, " then do your action. The group then responds by saying, "Hi, _____," and does your action. The person to the left goes next, saying his/her name and doing his/her action. The group repeats the name of the second person and does the action, then says your name and does your action. Keep going around the circle and repeating names and actions sequentially.

Variations: Switch places in the circle and do the names and actions again; connect all the movements together and do them by going around the circle as fast as the group can without stopping; make each movement as large as you can; then make each movement as small as you can.

Walking. Invite the group to walk around the room. Instruct them to change their stride in a variety of ways: Take longer steps, shorter steps, heavy steps, light steps, silly steps, and so forth. Next, describe situations and encourage the group to respond as if they were in that situation: (1) You are late for class/work. (2) You are trying to sneak up on someone. (3) You are sad that it is raining. (4) You are walking through the mud.

Action Songs. Sing and do actions to a song. Children's songs can be a fun way to release inhibitions ("Head Shoulders Knees and Toes," "If You're Happy and You Know It," etc.). Another possibility is to pick a favorite song or hymn and put actions to it. Invite the group members to sing and follow along with the movements you have created. This is not the time to teach a movement piece to a song, but to simply warm up. Therefore, if you are creating your own movements, pick simple actions like marching, clapping, and swaying.

Stretch to the Music. Choose a relaxing piece of music and stretch while it plays. Start with the head and do slow side-to-side movements, looking to the right, left, up, and down. Next do a few shoulder shrugs, lifting the shoulders to the ears and then pressing them down. Reach up with the arms and then slowly stretch up from side to side. Do six to eight arm circles forward and backward. Gently bend over at the waist. Hang upside down for a moment then bend and straighten your knees, trying to get closer and closer to the floor. Slowly come up one vertebrae at a time. Have the group lunge to each side to warm up the legs. Finally, warm up the feet by pointing and flexing the toes. Then do a few heel raises that progress into little jumps. Finally, invite the group to stretch anything they feel needs to be warmed-up.

Introducing Movement

By playing games that lead into movement, people will discover they are able to do liturgical movement. The purpose of the following activities is to provide nonthreatening experiences in order to introduce movement to the group. These activities are also helpful in getting creative ideas flowing.

Scarf Props

Supplies: a scarf or bandanna

Gather the group in a circle. Hold up a scarf. Demonstrate, by folding, twisting, or turning the scarf, how it can be made into something different (hat, parachute, belt, ice-cream cone, etc.). Invite the participants to take turns making the scarf into different props. Each time it is passed, the next person must make the scarf into something new and different. Start first and invite the participants to pass the scarf around the circle so that everyone gets a turn. You may give people the chance to pass and come back to them later if they need it. After going around once, try going around once more thinking of new ideas each time. If the group is ready for the challenge, see how many times they can pass the scarf around the circle as they create new props.

Scarf Dancing

Supplies: one scarf per person, strips of paper with patterns drawn on them

Before the group meets, draw line patterns on strips of paper (a wavy line, short dashes, spirals, zig-zags, etc.). Place the strips of paper on the wall or floor around the room. Give each person in the group a scarf or streamer to use. Ask participants to go to one of the strips of paper. Invite the participants to make the pattern they see on the paper with their scarf by waving the scarf through the air out in front of their bodies. Then have them enlarge their movements so they use the entire room to create their pattern.

Once people seem comfortable with this, ask them to join with another person or two. Each person should teach their partner their pattern. Then ask the partners to put the two patterns together. To make it more interesting, ask them to vary the speed or height of one or both of the patterns. Ask if any of the pairs would like to share their scarf dance with the whole group.

Talk to the Hand

This exercise was adapted from "Improvisation: Body Discovery" in *The Intimate Act of Choreography* by Lynne Anne Blom and L. Tarin Chaplin (see Resources, p. 82). Invite group members to look at their hand. Ask them to explore all the movements a hand can do (clap, slap, wiggle, snap, etc.). As you continue naming body parts (arm, leg, foot, etc.), have the participants discover all the ways the different parts of the body can move. Once they have had an opportunity to move their whole body, name an action (wiggle, tap, zoom, etc.) for them to do and the part of the body where the action will begin. For example, you would call out "Wiggle starting with your hand." The wiggle motion would begin in the hand, travel up the arm and throughout the rest of the body.

Next ask them to find a partner. Each person should think of an action (swing, shake, ooze, etc.) and a body part. One person starts their action and as it travels through the person's body the partner picks up the action and sends it through his/her body. One person might choose to shake. She/he could begin shaking her head, then arm, then maybe down the leg and to the foot. The partner would begin shaking their foot and send the shaking motion up their leg to their arm and head. When the shaking reaches his/her starting point, s/he can change the action and pass it back to his or her partner. Invite the group to change partners frequently.

Prop Walk

Supplies: scarf, blanket, broom, rope, stick, boxes

Collect a variety of items to be used as props (scarf, blanket, broom handle, rope, dowel rod, boxes). Ask each member of the group to select a prop. Invite them to use their prop as you tell a story. Tell any story you like as long as it can involve the whole group. For example, you are hiking in the mountains and all of a sudden it starts to rain. Each person should use their prop in any way they see fit (for example, a box could become an umbrella; a blanket could become a raincoat). You may also invite the group to tell the story by having each person say a line of the story.

Moving As a Group

Once a group has had an opportunity to warm up and be introduced to movement, it is time to have the group participate in activities that will allow them to start moving together as a whole group. The process of activities below starts with partners moving in pairs, then in groups of four, and finally as the whole group together. The process progresses from low-risk activities to higher-risk challenges where people are required to touch one another and trust each other to support their weight. Many of the activities are the same activities or variations on the activities that were done in chapter 2, but now we will use them as a lead-in to creating a liturgical movement piece.

Mirror, Mirror

(See p. 12 for complete instructions.)

If this activity is done with ease, challenge the participants to try to move as one unit. Encourage them to simply respond to the direction of the momentum of a movement with no one person leading or following.

Balancing

(See pp. 12–13 for complete instructions.)

If participants seem uncomfortable touching one another, make sure you do Body to Body and Move that Body (the next two activities) before moving to Sculpture Garden.

Body to Body

This exercise was adapted from *Dance and Elementary Education* by Ruth Lovell Murray (see Resources, p. 84). Tell group members that you are going to name two body parts. When you call out the body parts, each person should connect to one another by those parts. For example, if you say, "elbow to ear," then everyone must be connected to another person by either an elbow or an ear. Continue calling out body parts until groups seem to be more relaxed with one another. A good sign of people's comfort level is how much they are laughing and joking as the activity continues.

Move That Body

This exercise was adapted from *Dance and Elementary Education* (see Resources, p. 84). This activity is similar to Body to Body, but now when you say two body parts, add an action they must do while connected (walking, running, slithering, etc.). Remind participants to keep everyone safe. The object is not to create bruises but trust and communication.

Sculpture Garden

(See pp. 13–14 for instructions.)

Creating a Liturgical Movement Piece

The group has warmed-up, been introduced to movement, and moved as a group. It is time to create a liturgical movement piece to a specific Scripture passage.

Scripture Sculptures

(See pp. 14–16 for complete instructions.)

Once the group has begun moving on its own, you may want to make some suggestions as to where the audience is or remind them to move as one unit instead of individuals moving separately.

After the final reading, invite the participants to read the passage and spend three to five minutes meditating. Debrief the experience with the participants. Ask them to share their thoughts or feelings about the process of creating a liturgical movement piece. Ask them for their insights into the passage now that they have moved through it. Define what the message of the movement piece will be. Are there any other words they think are key to the message that they would like to add? Are there any words they would like to subtract now that the intent of the piece is clear?

Finalizing the Movement Piece

The group has now developed the basic structure of a movement piece. It is now time to refine the work that has been done. Begin the Scripture sculptures once more with the participants moving to the key words as the Scripture is read. Read the passage slowly and allow the participants to talk as they develop the sculptures. (The participants do not necessarily need to be connected to one another at this point.) Encourage the participants to think about the following:

- Think about the dynamics of the movement: fast or slow, strong or weak, large or small
- Experiment with the timing of entrances. Does the piece need to begin with one person on stage and the rest entering from other parts of the stage? Does the whole group need to enter together?
- Try small groupings of people all doing the same thing at the same time. Try it with everyone doing the same thing at different times. Try

everyone doing different movements at different times.

- Make sure the exit is choreographed. The last thing you want to do is perform a moving and meaningful liturgical movement piece only for movers to bump into each other as they try to leave the stage.
- Play, experiment, and have fun with the piece.
- Be open to the Holy Spirit working in your midst.

As the group rehearses, the movements should become consistent for each reading of the passage. Make sure the group is clear about what the purpose of the piece is and that the piece is communicating the message the group has chosen.

Stand back from the group and watch as another person reads. Ask yourself if the movements clearly communicate the intended message. Are the participants intentionally moving with focus and purpose?

Rehearse the piece several times and/or set up a rehearsal schedule. Work so that everyone is comfortable and able to do the whole piece together without stopping. Finally, before leaving, establish a rehearsal schedule that includes at least one rehearsal in the space where you will perform. The group will also need to consider costumes, props, lights, and sound. The following will give guidance on these matters.

Costumes should be kept simple. Consider who your audience is going to be and where the piece will be performed. If the piece is going to be performed in the sanctuary during worship, the participants may want to wear something that is comfortable to move in, but also does not stray too far away from the usual Sunday worship attire. We often suggest a plain shirt and a skirt or pants. This helps the congregation be more open and accepting, especially if the congregation is new to the art form.

It is a better picture on stage (most pleasing to the eye) if everyone is wearing something similar. The costumes should not detract from the movement, but enhance it. Also, consider if there is anyone in the movement piece whose costume should stand out or be in contrast with the others (an outcast might look different or someone portraying Jesus might wear a stole, etc.). Make sure the movers wear costumes that are flexible and can be moved in easily.

Props can also enhance a liturgical movement piece. Cloth is an excellent prop because it can be used in a variety of ways to enhance a liturgical movement piece. Because of its richness in texture and color, cloth can be used to represent just about anything. It can be water one moment and the wind the next. If you are doing a period piece (using costumes that people would wear at a particular time in history), you may want the participants to carry those objects that are part of that historical period.

Lights and sound can add dramatically to a movement piece. If you have the opportunity to perform on a stage with lighting and sound equipment, meet with the technical director and discuss the possibilities for your piece. If you are performing in a sanctuary, your lighting and sound options may be limited. However, make sure that the participants can be seen and the accompaniment can be heard by the entire congregation.

Debriefing

Creating a liturgical movement piece can be a very spiritual experience. We often only verbally express our feelings toward God. When we use our whole bodies to express God's Word and celebrate God's grace, it awakens our spirits and takes us to new levels of understanding. Make sure you allow for debriefing when the piece has been completed and/or performed. Encourage the participants to share their reactions to the liturgical movement development and/or performance. Discuss the following questions:

- What did you feel/think while going through the creative process?
- What did you feel/think while we performed the liturgical movement piece?
- Did you gain any new insights into the Scripture? into your faith?
- How does this experience relate to your life? to your relationship with God?

Experimenting with Movement

Once the group has been introduced to movement and moving together, you can begin exploring and experimenting with the different ways people communicate through movement. The purpose of the following activities is for the group to compare and contrast how they use movement to show emotions and actions. They will discover how each person in the group moves similarly or differently for a particular feeling or action. The group will also discover different, effective ways to communicate the message of a liturgical movement piece to an audience. If participants are going to meet on a regular basis, the activities also serve as a good way to keep choreography fresh and unique from one movement piece to the next.

Magazine Interpretation

Supplies: magazine pictures attached to construction paper

Before the group meets, collect pictures of people from magazines and newspapers. Select pictures that show people engaging in an activity, such as shooting a basketball, running away from someone, or driving a car. Also select pictures of sedentary activities, such as someone reading, spectators at an athletic event, or someone sleeping. Cut out the pictures and place them on pieces of construction paper to make them sturdier. Scatter the pictures on the floor or post them on the wall.

Ask the participants to look around the room and select a picture they like. Ask them to mimic whatever the person in the picture is doing. Once they have done that, ask them to create a short movement story that includes what the person in the picture is doing. Encourage the participants to show not only the person's movements, but also the emotions the person in the picture might be feeling. The movement stories should only be twenty to thirty seconds in length.

When they are done, invite each participant to find a partner. Each person should show their story to his or her partner. The partner can try to guess which picture the story came from. The partner should also watch how the person communicated with his or her body. Did they stomp when they were angry or cross their arms? Did they jump up and down when they celebrated or simply smile? Participants can then teach their partner their movement story. If time allows and people are willing, they can share their stories with the whole group.

Action Reaction

Supplies: pens/pencils, paper

Before the group meets, make a list of actions, such as walking, running, marching, and so forth. When you are making your list of actions, be sure to include actions that require little or no movement (such as "stop" or "freeze"). If you will be working with a particular Scripture passage later in the meeting, include words from the Scripture passage.

Ask participants to gather in the center of the room. Invite them to do the action that you call out. Have them explore and experiment with the movement by telling them to do it fast or slow, high or low, twisting or untwisting, and so forth. For instance, you could say, "Run quickly. Now slow it down until you stop."

Take a break from the movement and have them quickly write down in their initial reaction to the movement sequence. Have them answer the following questions:

- What were you thinking as you did the movement?
- What were you feeling as you did the movement?

- What kind of activity did the movement remind you of?

They might write, "I was thinking this is hard and I was feeling tired. It reminded me of a time when I missed the bus and I had to run to try to catch it, but was not able to."

Repeat the process until you have gone through your list of actions. Finally, reassemble the group and review their responses to the movement. Discuss the following questions:

- What actions did the group do (recount the list of actions)?
- What did you like best? least?
- What were you thinking or feeling as you did them?
- What kinds of activities did the movements remind you of?
- Invite people to share their way of doing a particular action. Compare and contrast the different movements to one word.

Flocking

This exercise was adapted from an exercise taught by Linda Graham Fallon at Hope College. It is a wonderful way to get a group to move together as a unit. Begin by gathering the group into a clump. They should be about a step apart from one another. Designate a leader to begin walking around the room. The group should stay clustered around the leader like birds do when they flock through the sky. While the group is still moving, call out another person's name and have them become the new leader. Encourage the group to make smooth transitions between leaders. It is more challenging for the group if you pick someone who is in the center of the cluster. If the group seems to do well with walking, invite them to quicken the pace.

Once everyone has had a chance to lead or you have switched leaders six or eight times, let the group flock on their own without you naming a leader. Have them try to follow the natural flow of the group.

After a few minutes, stop and review. Ask them how they felt while leading or following. Ask them if they have any suggestions on how the group might do it better. Give them an opportunity to try those suggestions.

Advanced Flocking

If the group has been together for a while or seems to be doing very well with flocking, they might want to try advanced flocking. Ask the group to resume the "clump" formation and begin flocking around the room. This time the flocking leader has the ability to change or add to the movement. For example, walking could lead into marching and marching could lead into stomping. As each new leader emerges, the movement can change. Before they begin, challenge them to try different levels and speeds and to use the whole room. If they find this difficult, you can always call out an action, but still allow them to find the natural leader.

Take some time to review. Ask again what it felt like to lead or follow. Did the movements flow together? Was there a dominant movement that kept recurring? Did participants feel like they were telling a story? What was the story about? How did they feel when it ended?

Basic Elements of a Liturgical Movement Piece

No matter how you decide to develop a liturgical movement piece, there are some basic elements that you must always consider. Whether you work alone to choreograph a movement piece or work with an entire group, you will need to consider the following seven elements. They are the pieces that hold the puzzle together.

People

It is important that you gather a group of people together who are willing to try new things and are invested in the project. The group may be the same group that did the experiential or deductive processes described in chapters 2 and 3, they may be a new group, or they may be a combination of both. Your group does not have to be composed only of dancers or people who look like "dancer types." The beauty of liturgical movement is that it is accessible to anyone: the "dancer type" or the person who thinks they are the most clumsy in the world; the artist or the person who doesn't remember the last time they did something artistic; the person who is comfortable on stage and the person who is not; the person who is able-bodied and the person who is physically challenged; the person who is young and the one who is older.

As you gather the group, make sure the expectations are clear. Is the group also the people who will perform? Can the group consist of people who will help plan and people who will help perform? How often will they meet? When is the date of performance? Be clear about goals and responsibilities, so that the group gathered will be the best group for the job.

Scripture Passage

In liturgical movement, as with any liturgical art, the movement (or art) is always rooted in God's Word. The art is a response to God's revelation to us through the Scriptures. Thus, a Scripture must be selected as one of the first activities you do or the group does together.

When selecting a Scripture passage, keep in mind that you will be

72

communicating the message primarily through movement. For people who are new to watching and/or performing liturgical movement, the more concrete a Scripture passage is, the easier it will be to interpret the movement. Jesus' parables, Old Testament stories, and the psalms provide a wealth of material to use for developing a liturgical movement piece. Also, if they are familiar with the Scripture passage, the people in the congregation will have an easier time understanding what is happening. Abstract Scripture passages (such as passages from Paul's letters or from parts of John's Gospel) can be communicated meaningfully, movingly, and beautifully through liturgical movement. However, they will be harder to work with because they are more abstract.

The Message

Discovering the message of a Scripture passage is a key element to liturgical movement. If liturgical movement is a response to the Word, then the Word must be studied. If you have gone through the experiential or deductive process for developing arts in worship (see chapters 2 and 3), you will have already worked to find the message in the Scripture. Start with one of the processes as a study of the Scripture. Also, discussing the following questions with your group can be very helpful, especially when considering a message to be communicated through liturgical movement.

- Does the passage tell a story? Determine the beginning, the middle, and the end. What happens during each section?
- Identify the mood of the passage. What are the people feeling? Who or what seems to be in control of the mood?
- Is there a particular emotional flow throughout the passage. Does it start out praising God and then end up angry? Or are people joyous throughout the whole passage?
- Look for the action that takes place in the Scripture passage. Does Jesus walk with the disciples? Do the people cry out to God for mercy? Think about who is doing the action in the Scripture passage. Who are the main and minor characters? If someone is talking, who is listening? If Jesus is doing the healing, who is being healed? What is the crowd doing?
- What metaphors are used in the passage? Do they have historical or cultural relevance (relevance to that particular place or time)? What is a similar metaphor that would have relevance to our modern day?
- What are the key words in the Scripture passage? Are they concrete or abstract? Are they full of action or full of emotion?
- What are the prominent images in the passages? Is it an object, such as

water? an emotion, such as fear? or a person, like Jesus?

After discussing all of the above, ask the group what is important to communicate about the passage. What is the message of the Scripture? Define clearly what the group's intention is for the liturgical movement piece. Determine what is the one message you want the congregation to understand by watching the liturgical movement piece. The task for the group will be to say that one message simply through movement. Try to get the message into one or two sentences. Write it out on a sheet of newsprint to help the group remember the purpose of the piece.

Accompaniment

Accompaniment is an additional element that supports or enhances the liturgical movement piece. One form of accompaniment is a *narrator*. With this form of accompaniment, it is important to be aware of the relationship between the reader and the movers. There is a rhythm. Decide who is leading and who is following. Help the reader understand where and how long to pause.

A second type of accompaniment is *music*. Someone can play an instrument or the music could be sung by a soloist or the whole choir. You can also use prerecorded music from a CD or tape.

A third type is the use of *sound effects*. Sound effects enhance liturgical movement by emphasizing a certain physical event (a thunderstorm) or a specific mood (sadness). For example, you could use the sound of a rainstorm, if you were telling the story of Jesus calming the storm (Matt. 8:23–27). If the movement piece focused on the days between Jesus' crucifixion and resurrection where a mood of sadness prevailed, you might choose to use a desert wind sound to emphasize the mood.

A final option is to perform the liturgical movement piece in *silence*. This can be a dramatic, striking accompaniment if it is used at the appropriate time.

Sequence

A liturgical movement piece should have a noticeable sequence. Liturgical movement is a way of telling a story. It should have a beginning, a middle, and an end. The congregation should be able to see the people take a starting position, communicate the message, and then find a final pose.

Form

The group will want to explore and choose the form of movement they would like to use to convey the message of the liturgical movement piece. The three movement styles are mime, movement, and dance. All three are art forms in and of themselves, but for the sake of this chapter we will use them to describe the way a person can communicate through a movement piece.

Mime

Mime, movement, and dance form a spectrum from concrete/literal to abstract. Mime is the most literal and concrete movement style. It is a reenactment of actual movements we make. For example, a person who wants to show someone praying might kneel and put their hands together with their head bowed.

Movement

Movement is between the literal/concrete and the abstract. A motion for prayer depends on the mood and situation of the one who is praying. If the person were praying for God to forgive them, he/she might stand with outstretched hands and arms reaching upward.

Dance

Dance is the most abstract movement style. A motion for prayer might include the whole body symbolizing two hands being brought together in prayer. A person might reach up with their arms and then contract inward with their head down. Then, they might reach out toward the audience.

Staging

It is important that you know where the liturgical movement piece will be performed before the group starts choreographing. Determine the opportunities and limitations of the space you will use.

Some sanctuaries are extremely flexible, where everything can be taken off the chancel. Some sanctuaries are harder to move in because the pulpit and communion table cannot be moved. These sanctuaries will create limits on the type of movements you can do. It is important to make sure the audience/congregation can see those people who are performing.

Notes to the Director

The director of liturgical movement, like the director of drama, is the person who is responsible for the big picture and how the small details contribute to the big picture. The director is the leader, organizer, coach, choreographer, and mood setter.

The director takes responsibility for the production of the piece by leading the group in creating a liturgical movement piece. The director needs to determine the needs and abilities of the people in the group. The experience of the participants will have a direct relation on how technical a piece you can expect them to form. The director can choose activities from this chapter to educate and improve on the abilities of the participants.

The director plays a very important role in choreography. If it is at all possible, the director should never be a part of the actual liturgical movement performance group. It is very difficult to be both dancer and choreographer. It will be difficult to keep your focus if you are worrying about exits and entrances of other people. Also, the director as choreographer needs to be able to step away from the group and look at the picture on stage. He or she needs to be able to watch the liturgical movement piece in action, so that he or she can look for what is working well and what needs to be changed. However, if you choose to perform in the piece, make sure you ask someone to observe the piece. This person can watch and give you another perspective.

The director is also responsible for handling the logistical aspects of performing the piece. The director/choreographer oversees all the activities that go into presenting the liturgical movement piece, from the actual staging to costumes to technical issues to publicity.

The director will need to make a rehearsal schedule, considering the time needed to complete the task and the schedules of those participating. He or she may want to work all in one day or over several one-hour sessions. When planning the session for creating a liturgical movement piece, allow time for breaks. People tend to be able to concentrate and focus for an hour before needing a break. If you break for more than fifteen minutes, you will need to warm up again.

The director will need to make arrangements for the dress rehearsal. Remember to reserve the performance space for the dress rehearsal. Rehearsing in the actual performance space will enable the group to get their bearings in the new space. If you have not had an opportunity to rehearse in the space, make sure the participants know how to make adjustments ahead of time. You can tape the dimensions of the performance space (be sure to include any obstacles such as pulpits, communion table, etc.) on the floor of your practice space. Also, check if you will be sharing the performance space or chancel with anyone or anything else (such as the choir, an ensemble of instruments, a baptismal font, etc.).

As with the director of a drama, the choreographer/director's greatest responsibility is setting the tone of the first rehearsal through the final presentation of the liturgical movement piece. The director is a minister to those with whom he/she works, and the director helps them to minister to each other. Again and again, our experience has been that ministry takes place through the process of creating, as well as the end result.

Tips in Teaching and Rehearsing Movement

When teaching and rehearsing liturgical movement, it is important to watch what the whole body is doing. In dance we look at the line the body is making in space. A "line" often runs from a person's fingers to the tips of his or her toes. Look for how all the body parts are moving in conjunction with one another. Don't forget minor body parts like shoulders and elbows, which can often distort a picture.

Also, look for what the whole group is doing. Remember your purpose for the piece. If everyone is supposed to be doing the same thing, make sure they are working together. If the group is doing synchronized movements, it is helpful to designate a leader for everyone else to keep in their peripheral vision.

You may need to teach the participants some basic movement principles. They should keep their shoulders down when they raise their arms. They should bend their knees when taking off on a jump and when they land. They should be aware of what their whole body is doing and not just their hands or arms.

Another important aspect to establish is focus. Where do people look? What is their motivation for looking where they do? Choose a focal point for God and keep it consistent throughout the entire piece. Make sure if you are gesturing to a certain place, like Jerusalem, that everyone points in the same direction. If they travel to or from that place, keep it consistent. Encourage participants to look out into the congregation unless they are doing a movement that calls for their head to be down. If people are nervous about looking into the congregation, give them a focal point that is slightly above the heads of the congregation.

Choreographing to Music

The process used to create a liturgical movement piece earlier in this chapter uses a Scripture passage. Contemporary Christian music or hymns are other excellent resources for liturgical movement. When choreographing a piece based on a song, follow the same process.

Do your research. Often a song or hymn is based on Scripture. Find the key words and images. Then use the sculpture process to get a basic form for your piece. Define the message you want to communicate. Finally, put the movements to the music. Using this process frees you to use symbolic movements and images. Remember, you do not have to have a movement for every word in the lyrics, just as you do not have to have a move for every word in a Scripture passage. Often trying to choreograph every word makes the movement piece confusing, unfocused, and awkward.

Evaluating

Before moving to the next liturgical movement piece or task, make sure the group has a time to evaluate the process, the performance, and the congregation's reaction. It is important that the group learn and grow from each experience they have together. Discuss the questions found on page 57 in chapter 6.

8

REFERENCES TO ARTS IN WORSHIP IN THE DIRECTORY FOR WORSHIP, PC(USA)

The content of this book reflects the theology and polity of the Presbyterian Church (U.S.A.). The Directory for Worship incorporates art as vital and important in the life of the congregation. Below are all the references to arts and worship found in The Constitution of the Presbyterian Church (U.S.A.), Part II, *Book of Order*, published by the Office of the General Assembly, Louisville, Kentucky, 1997.

The Language of Worship

[People] call God by name, invoke God's presence, beseech God in prayer, and stand before God in silence and contemplation. They bow before God, lift hands and voices in praise, sing, make music, and dance. Heart, soul, strength, and mind, with one accord, they join in the language, drama, and pageantry of worship. (W-1.2000)

Symbols spoken or acted are authentic and appropriate for Christian worship to the extent that they are faithful to the life, death, and resurrection of Jesus Christ. (W-1.2002)

The Use of Material in Worship

The Church has acknowledged that the lives of Christians and all they have belong to the Creator and are to be offered to God in worship. As sign and symbol of this self-offering, the people of God have presented their creations and material possessions to God. The richness of color, texture, form, sound, and motion has been brought into the act of worship. (W-1.3034)

Artistic Expressions

The Reformed heritage has called upon people to bring to worship material offerings which in their simplicity of form and function direct attention to what God has done and to the claim that God makes upon human life. The people of God have responded through creative expressions in architecture, furnishings, appointments, vestments, music, drama, language, and movement. When these artistic creations awaken us to God's presence, they are appropriate for worship. When they call attention to themselves, or are present for their beauty as an end in itself, they are idolatrous. Artistic expressions should edify, enhance, and expand worshippers' consciousness of the reality and grace of God. (W-1.3034)

The Session

In a particular church, the session is to provide for worship and shall encourage the people to participate fully and regularly in it. [The Session] is responsible . . . (h) for the use of special appointments such as flowers, candles, banners, paraments, and other objects of art, (i) for the overall program of music and other arts in the church, [and] (j) for those who lead worship through music, drama, dance, and other arts (G-10.0102d). (W-1.4004)

The Pastor

In a particular service of worship, the pastor is responsible for . . . (4) the music to be sung, [and] (5) the use of drama, dance, and other art forms. The pastor may confer with a worship committee in planning particular services of worship (G-6.0202). (W-1.4005)

Prayer

Song is a response which engages the whole self in prayer. (W-2.1003)

Instrumental music may be a form of prayer since words are not essential to prayer. In worship, music is not to be for entertainment or artistic display. Care should be taken that it not be used merely as a cover for silence. Music as prayer is to be a worthy offering to God on behalf of the people. (W-2.1004)

In the Old and New Testaments and through the ages, the people of God expressed prayer through actions as well as speech and song. So in worship today it is appropriate

a. to kneel, to bow, to stand, to lift hands in prayer.
b. to dance, to clap, to embrace in joy and praise,
c. to anoint and to lay on hands in intercession and supplication, commissioning and ordination. (W-2.1005)

Other Forms of Proclamation

The Word is also proclaimed through song. . . . Song in worship may also express the response of the people to the Word read, sung, enacted, or proclaimed. Drama and dance, poetry and pageant, indeed, most other human art forms are also expressions through which the people of God have proclaimed and responded to the Word. Those entrusted with the proclamation of the Word through art forms should exercise care that the gospel is faithfully presented in ways through which the people of God may receive and respond. (W-2.008)

Prayer in Personal Worship

One may take on an individual discipline of enacted prayer through dance, physical exercise, music, or other expressive activity as a response to grace. (W-5.4002)

In exercising the discipline of prayer in personal worship, one may find help for shaping the form and content of one's prayers . . . (b.) in hymns, spirituals, and other songs . . . (d.) in the heritages of prayer and devotion expressed in literature and visual arts. (W-5.4003)

9

RESOURCES FOR ARTS IN WORSHIP

The following is a list of resources that are helpful in developing an arts and worship group and ministry. Thanks to Paul Osborne of Atlanta, Georgia, for his significant help in putting this list together.

Most Important Resources

The Bible, the community of faith, their willingness to try something new, and hard work!

Other Helpful Resources

Atwood, Cory. *Banners for Beginners: A Step-by-Step Approach.* Ridgefield, CT: Morehouse Publishing, 1987.

Lots of "how-to," good for ideas.
Banbury, Gisela, and Angela Dewar. *How to Design and Make Banners for Sacred and Secular Festivals.* Ridgefield, CT: Morehouse Publishing, 1992.

A "how-to" book. Good for getting ideas.
Bennett, Gordon C. *Acting Out Faith.* St. Louis, MO: Chalice Press, 1986.

Comprehensive drama book. It has theory, history, categories, and how-to instructions.

Black, Don. *Do Something Different This Sunday: Biblical Comedies and Dramas for Youth and Adults.* Lima, OH: CSS Publishing Co., 1993.

Examples of scripts and modern adaptations of Scripture.
Blom, Lynne Anne, and L. Tarin Chaplin. *The Intimate Act of Choreography.* Pittsburgh: University of Pittsburgh Press, 1982.

Teaches the basics of choreography.
Brandt, Leslie F. *Epistles/Now.* St. Louis, MO: Concordia Publishing House, 1976.

A contemporary version of the letters in the New Testament.
—. *Prophets/Now.* St. Louis, MO: Concordia Publishing House, 1986.

A contemporary version of the prophets' writings.
—. *Psalms/Now.* St. Louis, MO: Concordia Publishing House, 1973.

A contemporary version of the Psalms.

Buchanan, Aimee Wallis, Bill Buchanan, and Jodi Martin. *Living in Community*. Bedford, VA: T.E.A.M., 1998.

A compilation of scripts for youth exploring the issues of living with the people around us, both in and out of the church, and how we might faithfully interact with them. To order, contact T.E.A.M. at 1125 Fairfield Rd. Bedford, VA 24523.

—. *Living in God*. Bedford, VA: T.E.A.M., 1998.

A compilation of scripts for youth exploring the identity of God and how God is revealed in our world today. To order, contact T.E.A.M. at 1125 Fairfield Rd., Bedford, VA 24523.

—. *Living in the Light*. Bedford, VA: T.E.A.M., 1998.

A compilation of scripts for youth focusing on the light of God and how we live in the light. To order, contact T.E.A.M. at 1125 Fairfield Rd., Bedford, VA 24523.

—. *Living in the Real World*. Bedford, VA: T.E.A.M., 1998.

A compilation of scripts for youth focusing on the struggle to remember who and whose we are and how we live as faithful Christians working for God's will in the world. To order, contact T.E.A.M. at 1125 Fairfield Rd., Bedford, VA 24523.

Cameron, Julia. *The Artist's Way*. New York: G.P. Putnam's Sons, 1992.

Provides a process that allows readers to gain a sense of who they are as artists, develop their own creative skills, and connect art to their faith.

Cappadona, Diane Apostolos, ed. *Art, Creativity, and the Sacred: An Anthology in Religion and Art*. New York: Crossroad, 1983.

Comprehensive theory, theology, and history of sacred art.

Cook, Jerry. *Worship Resources for Youth*. Champaign, IL: Crouse Printing, 1983.

Contains resources for worshiping with young people. Includes several practical ideas for using the arts in worship.

Davis, Donald. *Telling Your Own Stories*. Little Rock, AR: August House Publishers, Inc., 1993.

Good, simple theory about storytelling. Helps you develop your own stories.

Engstrom, W.A. *Multimedia in the Church: A Beginner's Guide for Putting It All Together*. Richmond: John Knox Press, 1973.

Gives a good basic understanding of video and audio in the church. Includes the technical aspects, though it is somewhat dated.

In Spirit and Truth: A Worship Book. Geneva, Switzerland: World Council of Churches, 1991.

The Worship Book from the World Council of Churches General Assembly, 1991. Includes calls to worship, prayers of adoration and confession, hymns, and liturgical responses from the global community.

Johnson, James Weldon. *God's Trombones.* New York: Penguin Books, 1990.

A series of Johnson's famous sermons in verse. Excellent to use in Reader's Theater, for monologues, or with liturgical movement.

Johnson, Martha. *Awesome Youth Sundays.* Louisville: Bridge Resources, 1997.

Guidance on creating a Youth Sunday. Includes ideas for arts in worship around seven different themes.

Knuth, Jill. *Banners Without Words.* Searcy, AR: Resource Publications, 1986.

Great ideas and designs.

Lawrence, Kenneth, ed. *Imaging the Word.* Cleveland: United Church Press, 1994.

Excellent resource for connecting art with lectionary. Lots of pictures/paintings. Connected with a curriculum and magazine.

Loder, Ted. *Eavesdropping on the Echoes: Voices from the Old Testament.* San Diego: LuraMedia, 1987.

Wonderful stories based on characters in the Old Testament.
—. *Guerrilas of Grace: Prayers for the Battle.* San Diego, CA: LuraMedia, 1984.

Beautiful prayers set in poems covering seven different subjects.
—. *Tracks in the Straw: Tales Spun from the Manger.* San Diego, CA: LuraMedia, 1985.

Stories and scripts based on the events surrounding Jesus' birth.
—. *Wrestling the Light: Ache and Awe in the Human-Divine Struggle.* San Diego, CA: LuraMedia, 1991.

A collection of poems and prayers covering six different subjects.

Murray, Ruth Lovell. *Dance and Elementary Education.* New York: Harper & Row Publishers, 1975.

Basics for teaching dance.

Nelson, Gertrud Mueller. *To Dance with God*. Mahwah, NJ: Paulist Press, 1986.

Contains theory and theology of worship. Explores ritual and celebration in the community of faith. Gives some art ideas for worship.

Nelson, Robin, and Tim Sloan. *1984 Puppet Training Seminar*. Produced by Bill Hawes, 1984.

Gives basic "how-to" on beginning a puppet ministry. No theory.

Perinni, Mary Paul Francis. *Creative Dramatics: A Guide for Educators*. New York: Herder & Herder, 1971.

Teaches basic concepts of drama. Written to be used with children, but can be adapted for other age groups.

Poovey, W.A. *Prodigals and Publicans*. Minneapolis: Augsburg Publishing House, 1980.

Six scripts based on biblical parables.

Rice, Wayne. *Up Close and Personal*. Grand Rapids: Zondervan Publishing House, 1989.

Excellent get-to-know-you and group-building activities especially designed for youth, but can be adapted for other age groups.

Karl, Rohnke. *The Bottomless Bag*. Dubuque, IA: Kendall/Hunt Publishing Company, 1991.

Full of get-to-know you and group-building/trust-building games.

—. *Silver Bullets*. Dubuque, IA: Kendall/Hunt Publishing Company, 1984.

The "Bible" of group initiative and trust-building games.

Rohnke, Karl, and Steve Butler. *Quicksilver: Adventure Games, Initiative Problems, Trust Activities, and a Guide to Effective Leadership*. Dubuque, IA: Kendal/Hunt Publishing Company, 1995.

A sister book to *Silver Bullets*.

Stanish, Bob. *Sunflowering: Thinking, Feeling, Doing Activities for Creative Expression*. Carthage, IL: Good Apple, Inc., 1977.

Great book to stimulate creative thinking.

Wangerin, Walter, Jr. *Ragman and Other Cries of Faith*. San Francisco: Harper & Row Publishers, 1984.

A book of short stories, scripts, and monologues focusing on the identity of Christ.

White, William R. *Stories for the Journey*. Minneapolis: Augsburg Publishing House, 1988.

First chapter is theory/rationale of storytelling. The rest is a collection of short stories to tell.

About the Authors

Aimee Wallis Buchanan writes for T.E.A.M. and other projects including curriculum, devotions, prose, and plays. She also travels with T.E.A.M. to lead youth conferences and worship workshops. Aimee holds a masters degree in Christian education from the Presbyterian School of Christian Education (1994) in Richmond, Virginia, and a masters of divinity degree from Columbia Theological Seminary (1996) in Decatur, Georgia. While not yet ordained, she is under care of Grace Presbytery and a member of Westminster Presbyterian Church (Arlington, TX) while also an affiliate member of Bedford Presbyterian Church (Bedford, VA) where she serves as a youth advisor. A Texan at heart, Aimee enjoys Mexican food and live music, especially if it's outdoors. She is crazy about her two-year-old daughter, Elli, and is devoted to their reading, giggling, and play sessions. She also loves to laugh hard and hang out with family and friends.

Bill Buchanan serves as the associate pastor for Bedford Presbyterian Church in Bedford, Virginia, where he holds primary responsibility for youth ministry and Christian education. He also leads the Presbytery Youth Council. He received a masters degree in Christian education from Presbyterian School of Christian Education in 1994 and a masters of divinity degree from Columbia Theological Seminary in 1996. Bill is originally from Raleigh, North Carolina, and grew up at White Memorial Presbyterian Church. This Tarheel is a dedicated college basketball fan, a gardener, an avid guitar player, and lover of all things musical. He, Aimee, and Elli live in a house in the country with a view of Virginia farmland and the Blue Ridge Mountains.

Jodi B. Martin divides her time between choreographing, writing, and traveling with T.E.A.M. and teaching for the Parent's Day Out program at First Presbyterian Church in Knoxville, Tennessee. Originally from Midland, Michigan, Jodi grew up at Memorial Presbyterian Church. It was there that Bev Kelly, the director of Christian education at that time, encouraged Jodi to attend Presbyterian School of Christian Education. Jodi graduated with a masters degree in Christian education in 1994. Jodi also holds a bachelors of arts degree in Dance and Psychology from Hope College in Holland, Michigan. While most of us are still sleeping in the morning, Jodi can be found jogging or roller blading around the neighborhood. She lives in Knoxville, Tennessee, with her husband Joe B. and her two very energetic children, Joseph and Benjamin.

About the Artist

The cover illustration, Celebration, was done by artist John August Swanson of Los Angeles, California. His works are found in the Smithsonian Institution's National Museum of American History and the National Museum of American Art, London's Tate Gallery, the Vatican Museum's Collection of Modern Religious Art, the Bibliotheque Nationale in Paris, and other public and private collections. The following are his reflections on this work:

All my life I have loved gatherings of people where there was a spirit of celebration and dancing. I went to dance troupe performances when they came to Los Angeles. The music and movements, as well as the colors and costumes, drew me in. This time, I began to make sketches of what I saw. I took the ethnic dances from the Middle East, Russia, Mexico, Sweden, Africa, East Asia, and India and the sacred dances of the Native Americans. I tried to learn everything I could about them. I love the whole array of dance performance: ballet, modern dance, jazz—especially the circus.

I started the acrylic painting of Celebration in 1996. I began to pull together a composite scene of every dance that has given me joy. I lit the scene with candlelight and starlight, making the beautiful garments glow. From the mosaic floor to the treelike arches that form the roof of the great hall, a mystical shimmer began to enter the picture.

Some sad events occurred in my family and interrupted the work, so I could only work sporadically. I found that, even with my misfortunes, working on the painting helped me to understand the events in my own life. When I finally finished the piece in February 1997, I looked on it as one of my favorite paintings.

I wanted to continue developing this image as a serigraph edition. I made it a larger piece, developing and enhancing it further. The changes grew through the slow, careful process of stenciling. I drew a separate stencil for each of the forty colors. The printed stencils built up layers of color and brought depth and a rich chiaroscuro of darkness and light. Jim Butterfield and I began the process in April 1997 and finished it in early November.

It has been an absorbing and rewarding task. I am happy to present to you my newest work.